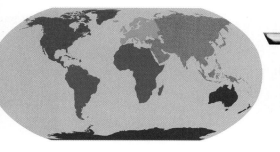

Table of Contents

How to Use the Atlas

Getting to Know Your World

An **atlas** is a collection of maps. This atlas is a collection of more than 90 physical, political, and thematic maps. It also includes photographs, charts, graphs, and other special features.

Physical Maps

On the physical maps, different **land elevations** and **ocean depths** are shown by different colors. Major **physical features**, such as the Rocky Mountains in North America, and major rivers, such as the Colorado River, are named. Countries and some cities are also named.

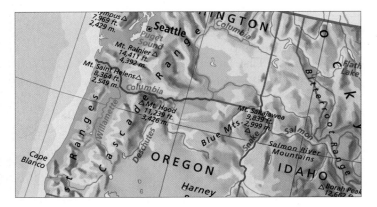

Political Maps

The political maps show **political units**—areas under one government, such as countries, states, provinces, territories, and cities. Countries, states, and provinces are shown in different colors so that you can recognize them more easily. Cities are shown in different sizes of type and have different symbols to show their populations.

Map Legends

The **legend** of a map explains the symbols used on the map. It helps you "decode" the information. In the atlas, the legends on the physical and political maps explain much of the map information. To keep the legends on the individual maps from getting too large, these legends include only a few key symbols. The complete legend for all information on the physical and political maps is on page 7. Take some time to get familiar with these symbols so that you can recognize them on the individual maps.

North America Physical Map

National capitals	Towns	Population
✪	■	Over 1,000,000
✪	▣	250,000 – 1,000,000
✪	•	Under 250,000
—		International boundary

Land elevation

3,000 meters —	— 9,480 feet
2,000 meters —	— 6,560 feet
1,000 meters —	— 3,280 feet
500 meters —	— 1,640 feet
200 meters —	— 656 feet
0 Sea level —	— 0 Sea level

Water depth

0 Sea level —	— 0 Sea level
200 meters —	— 656 feet
2,000 meters —	— 6,560 feet

0	200	400	600	800	1000 Miles

0	300	600	900	1200	1500 Kilometers

The **scale bar** in the legend tells how much smaller the map is than the real area it represents. The scale bar below is from the North America Political Map. see how the scale bar works, place your ruler on the You will see that one inch represents about 650 mil (one centimeter represents about 400 kilometers). Fin two cities on the map that are about one inch apart (or two cities that are about one centimeter apart) o the North America Political Map. In the real world, th places are about 650 miles (or 400 kilometers) apart

0	200	400	600	800	1000 Miles

0	300	600	900	1200	1500 Kilometers

Intermediate
World Atlas

Managing Editor
Brett R. Gover

Research and Writing
Elizabeth Leppman, PhD

Cartographic Coordination
Nina Lusterman

Cartography
Robert K. Argersinger, Gregory P. Babiak, Barbara Benstead, Marzee Eckhoff, Susan K. Hudson, Rob Merrill, David Simmons

Design
Rand McNally Design

Photo Credits

Cover images: © Photodisc; p. 8: bridge, desert, harbor, mountain © Photodisc; p. 16: globe, forest, swamp, crop and woodland © Photodisc; cropland © Corbis; crop and grazing land © Getty; p. grassland, barren land © Getty; desert, tundra, urban © Photodisc; p. 18: all photos © Photodisc; p. 19: Africa, Asia (1st) © Photodisc; Middle East © Getty; Asia (2nd) © Mason Florence/Lonely Pla Images; Australia © Corbis; p. 20: nomadic herding © Photodisc; hunting © Corbis; subsistence farming © Richard I'Anson/Lonely Planet Images; forestry © Getty; agriculture © Lindsay Brown/Lone Planet Images: p. 21: agriculture, stock raising © Photodisc; commerce, manufacturing, fishing © Getty: p. 24: earthquake © Getty: p. 25: eruption © Photodisc: p. 26: New Zealand © Gareth McCormack/Lonely Planet Images; Greenwich Observatory © Getty: p. 28: Mt. McKinley, San Francisco, pyramid © Photodisc; Parliament Hill © Cheryl Conlon/Lonely Planet Images; Greenland © De Swaney; cave art © Ingrid Roddis/Lonely Planet Images; corn © Corbis; Aztec art © Richard I'Anson/Lonely Planet Images; explorer © Getty: p. 29: New York © Rob Blakers/Lonely Planet Images; far Declaration, Canadian flag, American flag © Getty; Mexican village © Jeffrey Becom/Lonely Planet Images; sprawl © Jim Wark/Lonely Planet Images; Toronto © Jon Davidson/Lonely Planet Images; M Independence © Richard I'Anson/Lonely Planet Images: p. 32: Vancouver © Getty; Chicago © Ray Laskowitz/Lonely Planet Images; Havana © Jerry Alexander/Lonely Planet Images: p. 33: Pictured Ro Wellend Canal, flags, Alberta © Photodisc; Lake Michigan © Richard I'Anson/Lonely Planet Images; trawlers © Corbis; worker © Eric L. Wheater/Lonely Planet Images: p. 34: hurricane, Mexico City © Photodisc: p. 35: nuclear plant © Getty; Hoover Dam © Michael Aw/Lonely Planet Images; windmills © Photodisc: p. 41: Hawaii © Ann Cecil/Lonely Planet Images; Anchorage, pueblo ruins © Pho reservation © Gareth McCormack/Lonely Planet Images; dancer © Rick Gerharter/Lonely Planet Images: p. 43: immigrants © Getty; city, Alamo, Golden Gate Bridge, Corn Palace © Photodisc; Arch © Kaltenbach/Lonely Planet Images; Space Needle, Empire State Building © Getty: p. 46: Vermont farm © Mark Newman/Lonely Planet Images; lighthouse, New York © Photodisc; Mayflower, Niagara © Photodisc: p. 47: Capitol, Gettysburg, Atlantic City © Photodisc; Philadelphia © Richard Cummins/Lonely Planet Images; grist mill © Richard I'Anson/Lonely Planet Images: p. 48: Great Smokies, sp shuttle, Miami Beach © Photodisc; bayou © Olivier Cirendini/Lonely Planet Images; Charleston © Witold Skrypczak/Lonely Planet Images; Nashville © Richard I'Anson/Lonely Planet Images; Mississippi © Lee Foster/Lonely Planet Images: p. 49: farm © Richard Cummins/Lonely Planet Images; Chicago © Photodisc; sunflowers © John Elk III/Lonely Planet Images; St. Louis © Getty; corn © Corbis: p. ! Scotts Bluff © Alamy; cropland © Photodisc; circular field © Corbis; abandoned farm © Stephen Saks/Lonely Planet Images; Badlands © Carol Polich/Lonely Planet Images: p. 51: Dallas © Richard Cummins/Lonely Planet Images; Monument Valley © Izzet Keribar/Lonely Planet Images; White Sands NM © Carol Polich/Lonely Planet Images; Grand Canyon © Photodisc; Taos Pueblo © Andrew M & Leanne Walker/Lonely Planet Images: p. 52: Grand Tetons, Cliff Palace, Glacier NP © Photodisc; Bryce Canyon © Richard Cummins/Lonely Planet Images; Las Vegas © Richard Cummins/Lonely Plan Images: p. 53: flower farm © Richard Cummins/Lonely Planet Images; Hawaii © Photodisc; Alaska © Ernest Manewal/Lonely Planet Images; Seattle © Photodisc; Crater Lake © Roberto Soncin Gerometta/Lonely Planet Images: p. 58: Canadian Rockies, lighthouse © Photodisc: p. 59: scenic road, field of grain, fishing trawler © Photodisc; highway © Phillip & Karen Smith/Lonely Planet Imac Toronto © Glenn van der Knijff/Lonely Planet Images: p. 64: Mexico City © Richard I'Anson/Lonely Planet Images: p. 65: cactus, palm tree © Photodisc; rain forest © Tom Boyden/Lonely Planet Imag p. 66: Iguacu Falls © Judy Bellah/Lonely Planet Images; Buenos Aires, Machu Picchu © Photodisc; tortoises © Jeff Greenberg/Lonely Planet Images; Titicaca © Ryan Fox/Lonely Planet Images; explorer cane © Getty: p. 67: Amazon River © Greg Claire/Lonely Planet Images; Machu Picchu, Fitzroy NP, llamas, coffee beans, rain forest © Photodisc; Titicaca © Ryan Fox/Lonely Planet Images; children © Wheater/Lonely Planet Images; Buenos Aires © Getty: p. 70: parrot, rain forest © Photodisc: p. 71: Rio de Janeiro, rain forest © Photodisc; children © Bruce Yuan-Yue/Lonely Planet Images; São Paul © Paul Bernhardt/Lonely Planet Images; Cusco © Bruce Yuan-Yue/Lonely Planet Images; coffee plant © Chris Mellor/Lonely Planet Images: p. 72: Prague, church, column, Colosseum, Viking ship © G village, donkey, Stonehenge © Photodisc; iceberg © Corbis: p. 73: EU headquarters, euro, passports, David, gears, EU flag © Getty; sign © Jean-Bernard Carillet/Lonely Planet Images; Notre Dame © Photodisc: p. 78: England's Lake District © Paul Bigland/Lonely Planet Images; London © Getty; clock tower © Photodisc: p. 79: Matterhorn © Photodisc; Eiffel Tower © Getty: p. 80: Lisbon © Dc & Priscilla Alexander Eastman/Lonely Planet Images; Mt. Vesuvius © Christopher Wood/Lonely Planet Images; Roman coin, Amersterdam © Getty; train © Photodisc: p. 81: geothermal plant © Wade Eakle/Lonely Planet Images; dam © Grant Dixon/Lonely Planet Images; oil platform © Gareth McCormack/Lonely Planet Images; factory © Getty: p. 82: elephant, Sphinx, globe © Photodisc; Rift Vall © Matt Fletcher/Lonely Planet Images; lake and mountains © Patrick Horton/Lonely Planet Images; Ghana stool © Ariadne Van Zandbergen/Lonely Planet Images: p. 83: shepherd, EU headquarters © Mauritian women © Tom Cockrem/Lonely Planet Images; Egyptian children © Photodisc; Ethiopian girl © Ariadne Van Zandbergen/Lonely Planet Images; Liberian flag, African flags © Corbis; Sudan children © Damien Simonis/Lonely Planet Images: p. 86: rain forest, sand dunes, savanna, Johannesburg © Photodisc; Sahel © Jane Sweeney/Lonely Planet Images; oasis © Tony Wheeler/Lonely Plan Images; cropland © Christine Osborne/Lonely Planet Images: p. 87: elephants, gazelles, rhinoceroses, zebras © Getty; lion © Photodisc; cheetah and cubs © Alex Dissanayake/Lonely Planet Images: Suez Canal © Wayne Walton/Lonely Planet Images; dirt road © Photodisc; camels © Getty: p. 89: nomadic herding, ancient monuments, farming © Photodisc: p. 90: rice terraces, Great Wall © Pho Mt. Fuji © Bob Charlton/Lonely Planet Images; pinnacles, Taj Mahal © Getty; Mt. Everest © Corbis; Mesopotamian art © Jane Sweeney/Lonely Planet Images; T'ang tower © Bill Wassman/Lonely Pla Images: p. 91: Central Asia © Jane Sweeney/Lonely Planet Images; Southwest Asia © Olivier Cirendini/Lonely Planet Images; South Asia, Japanese flag © Getty; North Asia © Mark Newman/Lonely Planet Images; East Asia © Martin Moos/Lonely Planet Images; Southeast Asia, tsunami © Photodisc; oil derrick, India and Pakistan flags © Corbis: p. 92: Mt. Everest © Photodisc; Dead Sea © John Elk III/L Planet Images; Lake Baikal © John S. King/Lonely Planet Images; volcano © Corbis: p. 94: Indonesia © Gregory Adams/Lonely Planet Images; China © Phil M. Weymouth/Lonely Planet Images; Kyrgy © Anthony Plummer/Lonely Planet Images; Turkey © Getty: p. 102: rain forest © Photodisc; bridge © Juliet Coombe/Lonely Planet Images, rice farming © Patrick Ben Luke Snyder/Lonely Planet Imac auto plant © Getty: p. 103: Seoul © Photodisc; Bangladesh © Richard I'Anson/Lonely Planet Images; Mongolia © Justin Jeffrey/Lonely Planet Images: p. 104: bullet trains © Photodisc; road-building © Richard I'Anson/Lonely Planet Images; Nepal © Anders Blomqvist/Lonely Planet Images; Mongolian steppe © Paul Greenway/Lonely Planet Images: p. 105: oil refinery © Getty; tanker and pipeline © Corbis: p. 106: Uluru © Chris Mellor/Lonely Planet Images; Sydney, Northern Territory, flag, gold © Getty; cattle and mountains © Fergus Blakiston/Lonely Planet Images; Aboriginal art © Photodi p. 107: koala © Photodisc; wallabies, Tasmanian devil, wombat, ballot box, flag, Olympic medals © Getty; Aborigine © Corbis: p. 110: snowy trees © Rob Blakers/Lonely Planet Images; road sign © Napthine/Lonely Planet Images; Pinnacles Desert © Photodisc; grassland © Paul Sinclair/Lonely Planet Images; rain forest © Russell Mountford/Lonely Planet Images; cattle and sheep © David Wall/Lo Planet Images: p. 111: sheep © Getty; wrasse © Robert Halstead/Lonely Planet Images; shark © Leonard Douglas Zell/Lonely Planet Images; coral © Michael Aw/Lonely Planet Images; island © Peter Hendrie/Lonely Planet Images: p. 114: kayakers © Juliet Coombe/Lonely Planet Images; icebreaker © Corbis; crevasse © Scott Darsney/Lonely Planet Images; Antarctic coast © Chris Barton/Lonely Pla Images; Victoria Land © Jonathon Chester/Lonely Planet Images; Amundsen © Holger Leue/Lonely Planet Images; airplane © Getty: p. 115: ice-drilling © David Etheridge/Lonely Planet Images; wea monitoring © David Etheridge/Lonely Planet Images; orcas, albatross, penguins, iceberg © Corbis; seal, Wellington Agreement © Getty; IGY © David Etheridge/Lonely Planet Images; Antarctic Treaty © David Etheridge/ Lonely Planet Images

Printed in the United States of America

Rand McNally & Company
Skokie, Illinois 60076-8906

ISBN: 528-93460-0

10 9 8 7 6 5 4 3 2 1

For information about ordering the *Intermediate World Atlas*, call 1-800-678-RAND (-7263) or visit our website at **www.randmcnally.com**.

...ectional Arrows

...e physical and political maps in this atlas have ...ectional arrows. The four arrows together are called a **compass rose**. The letters on the compass rose ...nd for **North**, **South**, **East**, and **West**. On the map, the ...rth arrow always points toward the North Pole. ...e South arrow always points toward the South Pole.

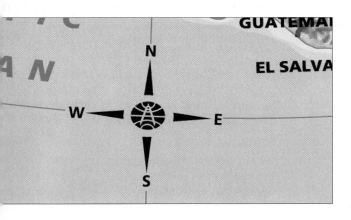

...p Grids

...e blue lines drawn east-west across the maps are ...es of **latitude**, or parallels. The blue lines drawn ...th-south are **lines of longitude**, or meridians. The ...es of latitude and longitude create **grids** on the maps.

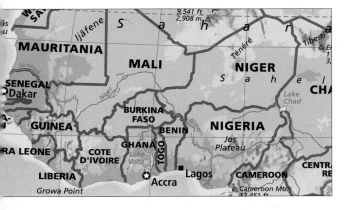

...e physical and political maps have red letters along ...h sides and red numbers along the top and bottom. ...ese letters and numbers are one way of giving ...mes to these grids.

Look at the political map of Africa on page 85. Put your left index finger on the **E** at the left side of the map, and your right index finger on the **4** at the top of the map. Trace both fingers across the map until they meet at the grid square where the city of Lagos, Nigeria, is located.

Lagos is in the **E4** square of the grid on the map. The lines of latitude north and south of the E and the lines of longitude on either side of the 4 create the E4 square. (See the areas highlighted in purple on the map below.) E4 is the map key, or alpha-numeric grid location, for Lagos. What other cities are in the E4 square?

The city of Mogadishu in Somalia is in the E8 square. In what square do you find the country of Sierra Leone?

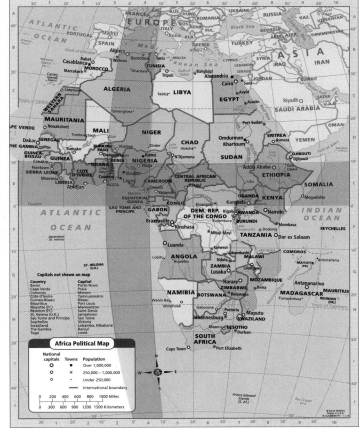

Index

The index is **a list in alphabetical order** of most of the places that appear on the maps. Each place entry in the index is followed by its map key, or alpha-numeric grid location, and the number of the page on which it appears.

Place	Map Key	Page
A		
Aberdeen, *South Dakota*	B6	38
Abidjan, *cap. Cote d'Ivoire, Afr.*	E3	85
Abilene, *Texas*	E6	38
Absaroka Range, *U.S.*	B3	36
Abu Dhabi, *cap. U. A. Emirates, Asia*	C5	97
Abuja, *cap. Nigeria, Afr.*	E4	85
Acapulco, *Guerrero, Mexico*	C3	62
Accra, *cap. Ghana, Afr.*	E3	85
Aconcagua, *Cerro, highest peak, S.A.*	G4	68
Adana, *Turkey*	B3	96
Ad-Dammām, *Saudi Arabia*	C5	96
Addis Ababa, *cap. Ethiopia, Afr.*	E7	85
Adelaide, cap. South Australia		

Place
Amu Darya, *river, A.*
Amundsen Sea, *Ant.*
Amur River, *Asia*
Anchorage, *Alaska.*
Andaman Islands, *In*
Andes, *mts., S.A.*
Andorra, *country, E*
Angara River, *Russia*
Angarsk, *Russia*
Angel Falls, *S.A.*
Angola, *country, Af*
Anguilla, *dep., N.A.*
Anhui, *province, Ch*
Ankara, *cap. Turkey*
Ann Arbor, *Michiga*
Annapolis, *cap. Mar*

Thematic Maps

Have you ever seen a weather map on television that uses different colors to show places with different temperatures? That map is a thematic map. It shows information about **a specific topic** and where a particular condition is found. The thematic maps in this atlas give you information about specific topics or themes.

This atlas has ten world thematic maps. These maps let you compare the same kinds of information for areas around the world. For example, you could use the World Climate Map to see what places in the world have a climate similar to the climate where you live.

This atlas also has thematic maps in the sections about each of the continents. Several different thematic maps appear on the same page. This allows you to compare different topics for the same area. For example, if you compare a climate map and a population density map for Africa, what do you think you might discover?

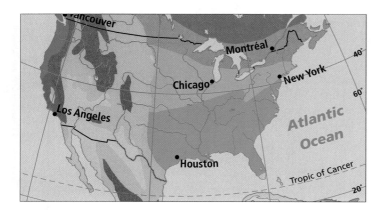

Did you know?

Each "Did You Know?" presents an interesting fact about the world.

What If?

Each "What If?" asks you to use information from the atlas and other sources to answer a critical thinking question. There are no right or wrong answers, but be sure you can present facts to support your opinions.

Graphs, Charts, and Photographs

The graphs, charts, and photographs in the atlas help illustrate information from the maps. They may help you see the same information in a different way. They may also provide additional information about the themes of the maps. The photographs will show you how the features shown on the map look in the real world.

World Lumber Exports

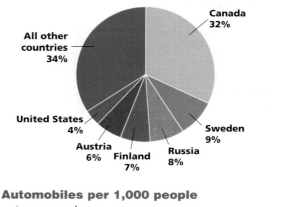

Automobiles per 1,000 people

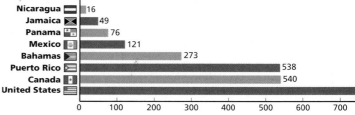

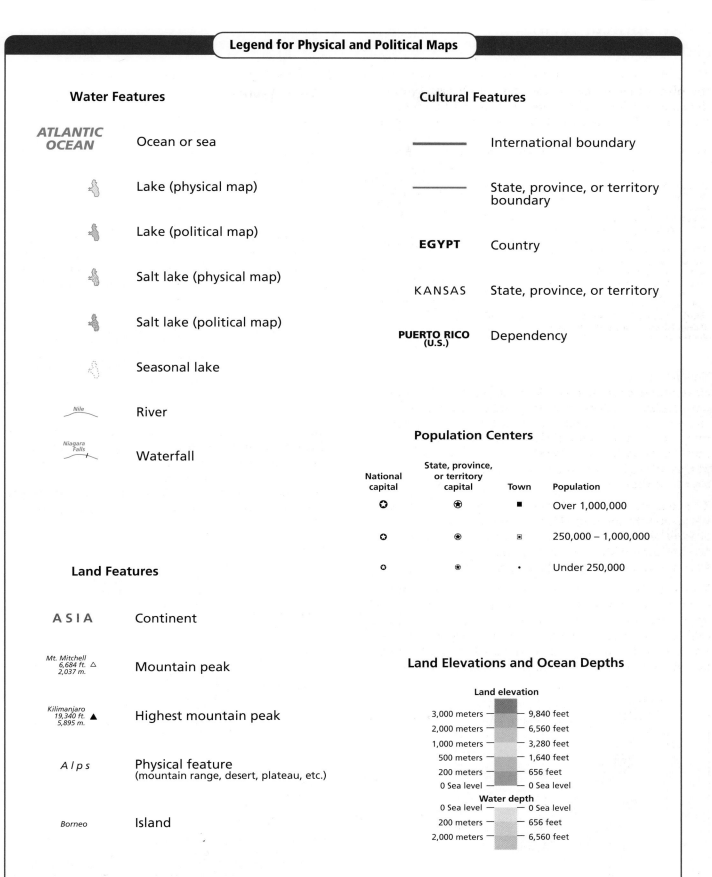

Legend for Physical and Political Maps

Water Features

ATLANTIC OCEAN Ocean or sea

Lake (physical map)

Lake (political map)

Salt lake (physical map)

Salt lake (political map)

Seasonal lake

Nile River

Niagara Falls Waterfall

Land Features

ASIA Continent

Mt. Mitchell 6,684 ft. 2,037 m. △ Mountain peak

Kilimanjaro 19,340 ft. 5,895 m. ▲ Highest mountain peak

Alps Physical feature (mountain range, desert, plateau, etc.)

Borneo Island

Cultural Features

⸻ International boundary

⸺ State, province, or territory boundary

EGYPT Country

KANSAS State, province, or territory

PUERTO RICO (U.S.) Dependency

Population Centers

National capital	State, province, or territory capital	Town	Population
✪	✸	■	Over 1,000,000
✪	✸	▣	250,000 – 1,000,000
✪	✸	·	Under 250,000

Land Elevations and Ocean Depths

Land elevation

3,000 meters	9,840 feet
2,000 meters	6,560 feet
1,000 meters	3,280 feet
500 meters	1,640 feet
200 meters	656 feet
0 Sea level	0 Sea level

Water depth

0 Sea level	0 Sea level
200 meters	656 feet
2,000 meters	6,560 feet

Geographical Terms

The large illustration to the right is a view of an imaginary place. It shows many of Earth's different types of landforms, bodies of water, and political features. The following vocabulary list defines many of the features on the map. *

See if you can find an example of each feature on the maps in the atlas.

Archipelago:
A group of islands.

Canyon:
A deep, narrow valley with high, steep sides.

Coast:
Land along a large lake, a sea, or an ocean.

Desert:
A large land area that receives very little rainfall.

Forest:
A large area covered with trees.

Gulf:
A large part of an ocean or a sea that lies within a curved coastline. A gulf is larger than a bay.

Harbor:
A sheltered body of water where ships can safely anchor.

Hill:
A small area of land that is higher than the land around it.

Island:
A piece of land that is surrounded by water.

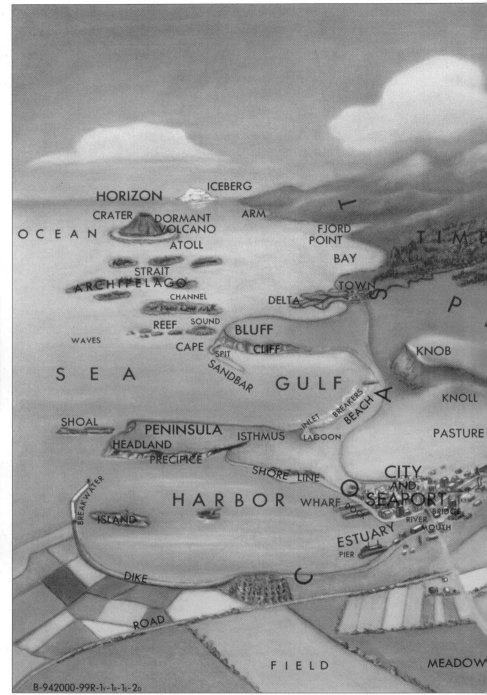

Isthmus:
A narrow piece of land that joins two larger areas of lar

Lake:
A body of water completely surrounded by land.

Mountain:
Land that rises much higher than the land around it.

* The Rand McNally Geographical Terms Desk Map (order number 005-13156-1)   includes definitions for all of the terms that appear

ountain range:
ow of mountains that are joined together.

ean:
e of Earth's largest bodies of water.

in:
rge, flat land area.

teau:
rge area of land where the highest elevation is generally
same. A plateau may have deep valleys.

River:
A body of fresh water that flows from higher to lower land.
A river usually flows into another river, a lake, a sea, or
an ocean.

Sea:
A large body of salt water nearly or partly surrounded
by land. A sea is much smaller than an ocean.

Valley:
Lower land between hills or mountains.

World Physical Map

This map shows the world's land elevations and ocean depths.

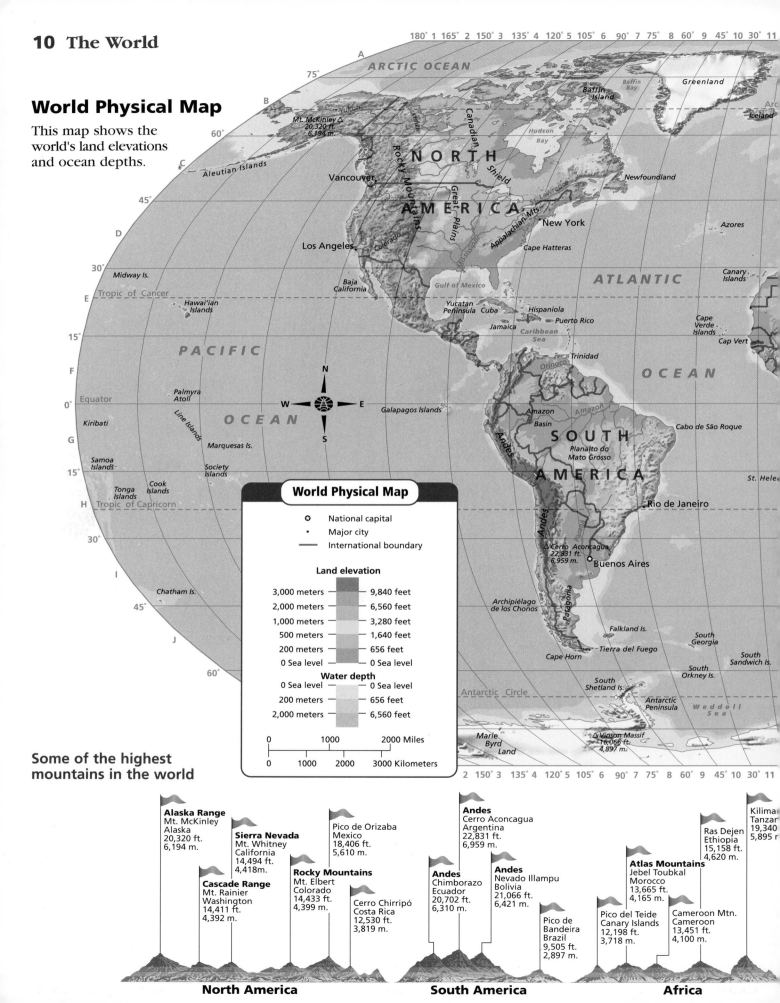

Some of the highest mountains in the world

14 30° 15 45° 16 60° 17 75° 18 90° 19 105° 20 120° 21 135° 22 150° 23 165° 24 180°

ARCTIC OCEAN

A

75°

Franz
Josef Land

Nordkapp

Novaya
Zemlya

B

andinavia

S i b e r i a

60°

Bering
Sea

Moscow

Volga

Ural Mts.

Yenisey

Ob

C

45°

Don

Sea of Okhotsk

Kamchatka
Peninsula

Sakhalin

A S I A

Altai Mts.

Balkan
Peninsula

Caucasus
△Gora El'brus
18,510 ft.
5,642 m.

Black Sea

Aral

Pamir

Gobi Desert

Hokkaidō

D

45°

Sicily

Crete

Cyprus

Zagros Mts.

Beijing

Sea of Japan

Honshū

Cairo

Plateau
of
Tibet

Himalayas

Huang

Yangzi

East
China
Sea

Kyūshū

30°

hara

Nile

Red Sea

Arabian
Peninsula

Ganges

Indus

▲Mt. Everest
29,028 ft
8,848 m.

Taiwan

PACIFIC

Tropic of Cancer

E

15°

ICA

el

Mumbai
(Bombay)

Deccan

Hainan Dao

South China
Sea

Luzon

Mariana
Islands

Wake
Island

Arabian
Sea

Socotra

Bay of
Bengal

Malay
Peninsula

Mindanao

Palau
Islands

Guam

OCEAN

Lakshadweep

Sri Lanka

Caroline
Islands

Marshall
Islands

F

0°

Maldive
Islands

Borneo

Celebes

Equator

△Kilimanjaro
19,340 ft.
5,895 m.

Seychelles

Sumatra

Java

New Guinea

Solomon
Islands

Congo
Basin

Rift Valley

Cocos
Islands

G

15°

Zambezi

INDIAN

Madagascar

Mauritius

Coral Sea

New
Hebrides

New Caledonia

Fiji
Is.

Kalahari
Desert

Reunion

Great
Sandy
Desert

A U S T R A L I A

Tropic of Capricorn

H

30°

Good Hope

Johannesburg

OCEAN

Great Dividing Range

Darling

Sydney

Cape Leeuwin

Aoraki
(Mt. Cook)
12,316 ft.
3,754 m. △

North Island

I

aud

Îles Kerguélen

Tasmania

South Island

45°

OUTHERN

OCEAN

J

60°

Antarctic Circle

Enderby
Land

Wilkes Land

K

75°

NTARCTICA

Victoria Land

© Rand McNally
Made in U.S.A.
N-CLA10000-A1- -4- -6

L

14 30° 15 45° 16 60° 17 75° 18 90° 19 105° 20 120° 21 135° 22 150° 23 165° 24 180°

Pyrenees
Aneto
Spain
11,168 ft.
3,404 m.

Alps
Mont Blanc
France-Italy
15,771 ft.
4,807 m.

Caucasus
Gora El'brus
Russia
18,510 ft.
5,642 m.

Monte Etna
Italy
10,902 ft.
3,323 m.

kla
land
92 ft.
91 m.

Galdhøpiggen
Norway
8,100 ft.
2,469 m.

Pamirs
Pik Imeni
Ismail Samani
Tajikistan
24,590 ft.
7,495 m.

Elburz Mts.
Kūh-e
Damāvand
Iran
18,386 ft.
5,604 m.

Himalayas
K2
China-India
28,250 ft.
8,611 m.

Himalayas
Mt. Everest
China-Nepal
29,028 ft.
8,848 m.

Himalayas
Kānchenjunga
Nepal-India
28,208 ft.
8,598 m.

Fuji-san
Japan
12,388 ft.
3,776 m.

Gongga Shan
China
24,902 ft.
7,590 m.

Vulkan Klyuchevskaya
Sopka
Russia
15,584 ft.
4,750 m.

Gunong
Kinabalu
Malaysia
13,455 ft.
4,101 m.

Puncak Jaya
Indonesia
16,503 ft.
5,030 m.

Mt. Kosciuszko
Australia
7,313 ft.
2,229 m.

Mt. Wilhelm
Papua New Guinea
14,793 ft.
4,509 m.

Mauna Kea
Hawaii
13,796 ft.
4,205 m.

Aoraki (Mt. Cook)
New Zealand
12,316 ft.
3,754 m.

Europe

Asia

Australia and Oceania

World Political Map

People have divided up Earth's land into almost 200 countries. A few of these countries are more than a thousand years old, but most have formed in the last 200 years.

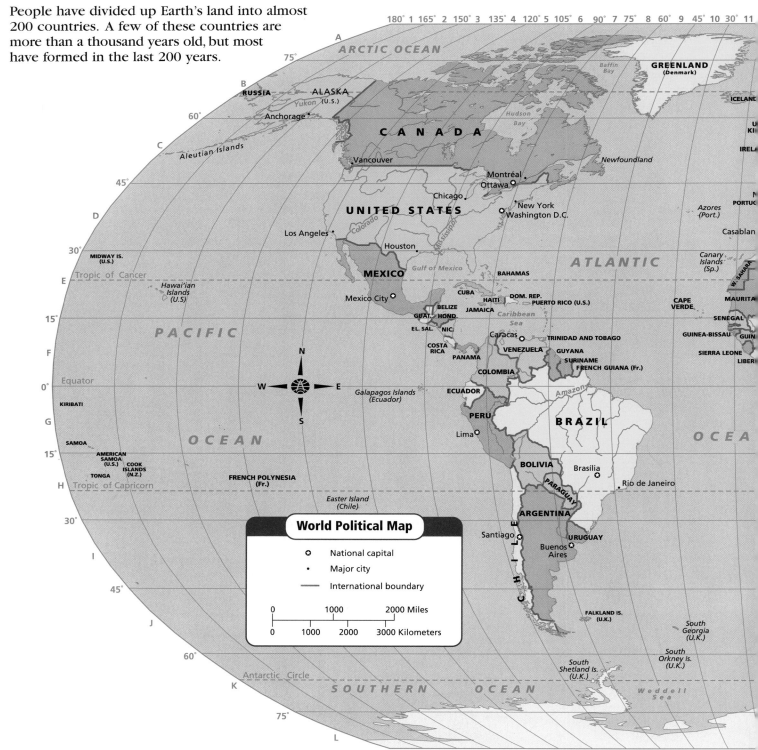

World Political Map

⊛ National capital

• Major city

— International boundary

0   1000   2000 Miles

0   1000   2000   3000 Kilometers

14 30° 15 45° 16 60° 17 75° 18 90° 19 105° 20 120° 21 135° 22 150° 23 165° 24 180°

Franz Josef Land

ARCTIC OCEAN A

75°

Novaya Zemlya

B

FINLAND

R U S S I A 60°

Bering Sea

SWEDEN EST.
LAT.
LITH. •Moscow *Volga* •Novosibirsk *Sea of Okhotsk* C

ANY POLAND BELARUS
UKRAINE KAZAKHSTAN MONGOLIA 45°

AUS. HUNG.
CRO. SLVK.
BOS. MOLD.
ALB. ROM.
BUL UZBEKISTAN KYRG. NORTH
KOREA *Sea of Japan*
D
GREECE GEO.
ARM. AZER. TURKMENISTAN TAJIK. Beijing• JAPAN
TURKEY CHINA Seoul• SOUTH
KOREA Tōkyō•

NISIA *Black Sea* CYPRUS SYRIA LEB.
ISRAEL IRAQ AFGHANISTAN *Yangtze* Shanghai• 30°
Crete JORDAN IRAN NEPAL BHU. PACIFIC
LIBYA EGYPT KUWAIT PAKISTAN *Ganges* BNGL. TAIWAN *Tropic of Cancer* E
Cairo• SAUDI QATAR Karáchi• Kolkata MYANMAR Hong Kong• NORTHERN
MARIANA ISLANDS
(U.S.) WAKE ISLAND
(U.S.)
ARABIA U.A.E. (Calcutta) LAOS
Mumbai INDIA THAILAND *South China* 15°
ER CHAD OMAN (Bombay)• *Arabian* *Bay of* Bangkok• VIETNAM Manila• PHILIPPINES GUAM OCEAN
SUDAN YEMEN *Sea* *Bengal* CAMBODIA *Sea* (U.S.)
IA Addis DJIBOUTI SRI LANKA PALAU
Ababa• BRUNEI FED. STATES OF F
ROON CENTRAL
AFRICAN
REPUBLIC ETHIOPIA MALDIVES MALAYSIA MICRONESIA MARSHALL
ISLANDS
ABON UGANDA SOMALIA SINGAPORE *Borneo* *New Guinea* 0°
RWANDA KENYA SEYCHELLES *Equator*
DEM. REP.
OF THE CONGO BURUNDI *Sumatra* •Jakarta INDONESIA PAPUA SOLOMON
TANZANIA *Java* EAST TIMOR NEW GUINEA ISLANDS G

ANGOLA INDIAN 15°
ZAMBIA COMOROS *Coral Sea* VANUATU
MADAGASCAR MAURITIUS NEW CALEDONIA FIJI
NAMIBIA ZIMBABWE REUNION (Fr.)
BOTSWANA (Fr.) *Tropic of Capricorn* H
Johannesburg• OCEAN AUSTRALIA Brisbane•

SWAZILAND Perth• *Darling* Sydney• 30°
SOUTH LESOTHO
AFRICA Melbourne• Auckland•
NEW ZEALAND I

Tasmania

45°
Îles Kerguélen
(Fr.)
J

SOUTHERN OCEAN 60°
Antarctic Circle
K

NTARCTICA © Rand McNally
Made in U.S.A.
N-CLA10000-P1- -7-8-9 75°
L

14 30° 15 45° 16 60° 17 75° 18 90° 19 105° 20 120° 21 135° 22 150° 23 165° 24 180°

World Climate Map

This map shows climate conditions throughout the world. Climate is the average **weather conditions** over a long period of time. Temperature and precipitation together make up climate.

Climate Graphs

Each of the climate graphs below shows the average temperature and precipitation for every month of the year. The 12 letters below each graph are the first letters of the twelve months, beginning with January (J) and ending with December (D). There is one climate graph for every type of climate region in the world.

Curved lines on the graphs show temperatures in degrees Celsius and degrees Fahrenheit. The numbers are to the left of the graphs.

Vertical bars on the graphs show monthly precipitation in inches and centimeters. The numbers are to the right of the graphs.

Colors on the graphs match colors on the map. The cities for the graphs are also shown on the map.

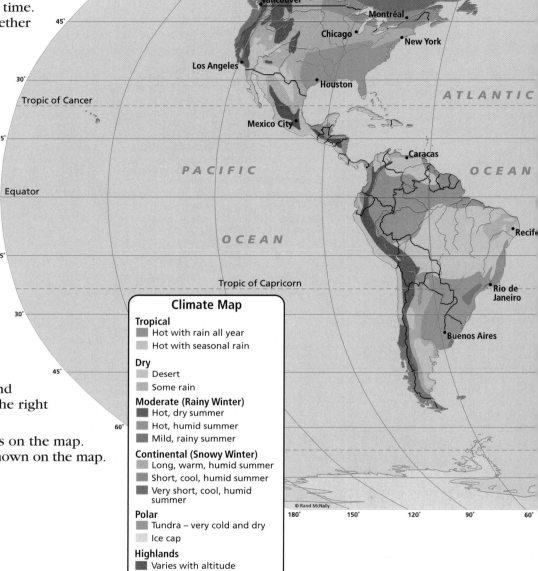

Climate Map

Tropical
Hot with rain all year
Hot with seasonal rain

Dry
Desert
Some rain

Moderate (Rainy Winter)
Hot, dry summer
Hot, humid summer
Mild, rainy summer

Continental (Snowy Winter)
Long, warm, humid summer
Short, cool, humid summer
Very short, cool, humid summer

Polar
Tundra – very cold and dry
Ice cap

Highlands
Varies with altitude

© Rand McNally

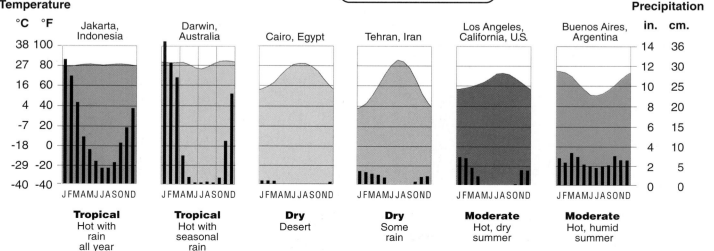

Temperature   **Precipitation**

| Jakarta, Indonesia | Darwin, Australia | Cairo, Egypt | Tehran, Iran | Los Angeles, California, U.S. | Buenos Aires, Argentina |

Tropical
Hot with rain all year

Tropical
Hot with seasonal rain

Dry
Desert

Dry
Some rain

Moderate
Hot, dry summer

Moderate
Hot, humid summer

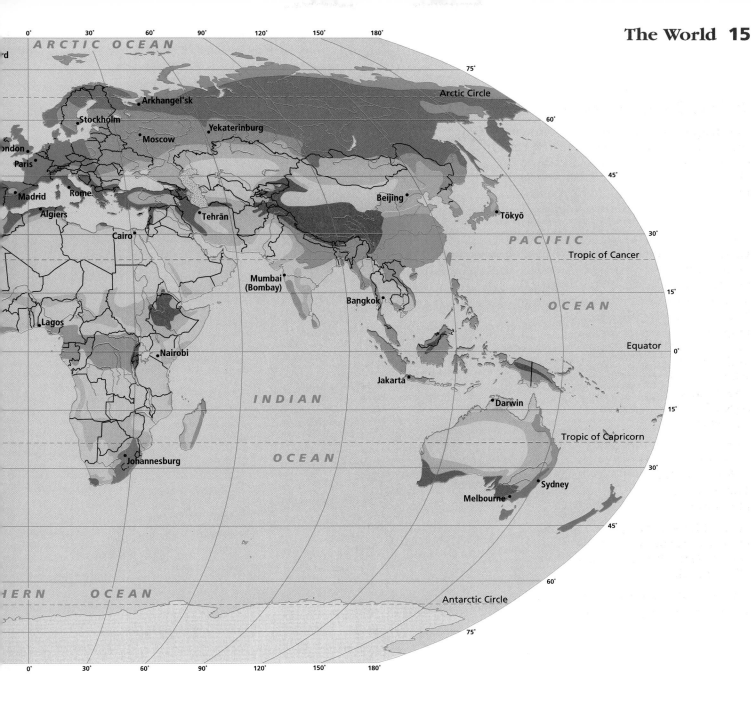

ARCTIC OCEAN

Arctic Circle

Arkhangel'sk

Stockholm
Moscow
Yekaterinburg

London
Paris

Madrid
Rome
Algiers
Beijing
Tōkyō

PACIFIC

Cairo
Tehrān

Tropic of Cancer

Mumbai
(Bombay)

OCEAN

Bangkok

Lagos

Nairobi

Jakarta
Equator

INDIAN
Darwin

OCEAN
Tropic of Capricorn

Johannesburg
Sydney
Melbourne

HERN   OCEAN

Antarctic Circle

Temperature   **Precipitation**

°C   °F   in.   cm.

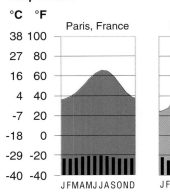

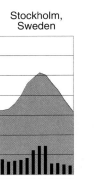

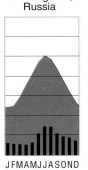

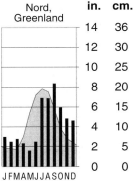

38	100
27	80
16	60
4	40
-7	20
-18	0
-29	-20
-40	-40

Paris, France

Chicago,
Illinois, U.S.

Stockholm,
Sweden

Arkhangel'sk,
Russia

Barrow,
Alaska, U.S.

Nord,
Greenland

14	36
12	30
10	25
8	20
6	15
4	10
2	5
0	0

JFMAMJJASOND   JFMAMJJASOND   JFMAMJJASOND   JFMAMJJASOND   JFMAMJJASOND   JFMAMJJASOND

Moderate
Mild,
rainy
summer

Continental
Long, warm,
humid summer

Continental
Short, cool,
humid summer

Continental
Very short,
cool, humid
summer

Polar
Tundra
very cold
and dry

Polar
Ice cap

World Environments Map

This map shows different environments throughout the world. The environment of a place is its physical setting and conditions. Some environments, such as forest and tundra, are natural. Other environments, such as cropland and urban areas, have been created by humans. This map shows many of the world's largest urban areas.

The theme of this map is land environments, but 75% of Earth's surface is covered by water. This causes Earth to look blue from space. For this reason, Earth is sometimes called the Blue Planet. Only 3% of the water on Earth is fresh water. The other 97% of Earth's water is salt water.

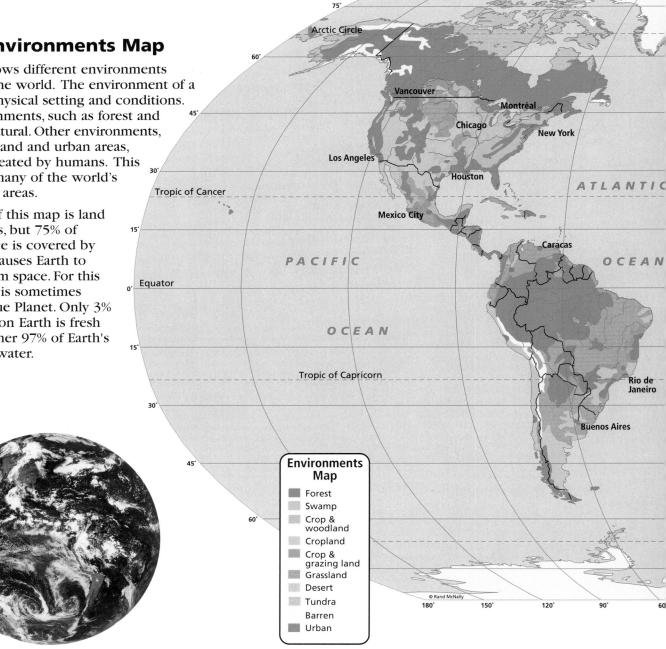

Environments Map

- Forest
- Swamp
- Crop & woodland
- Cropland
- Crop & grazing land
- Grassland
- Desert
- Tundra
- Barren
- Urban

© Rand McNally

Forest

Swamp

Crop and woodland

Cropland

Crop and grazing land

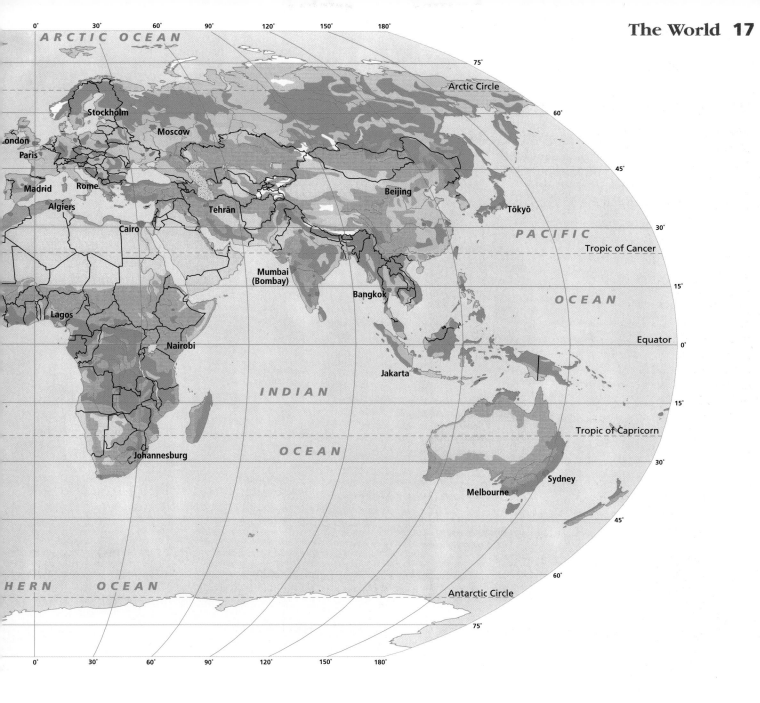

ARCTIC OCEAN

75°

Arctic Circle

60°

Stockholm

Moscow

45°

London

Paris

Beijing

Tōkyō

Madrid

Rome

PACIFIC

30°

Algiers

Tehrān

Cairo

Tropic of Cancer

15°

Mumbai
(Bombay)

OCEAN

Lagos

Bangkok

Nairobi

Equator 0°

Jakarta

INDIAN

15°

OCEAN

Tropic of Capricorn

Johannesburg

Sydney

30°

Melbourne

45°

60°

HERN OCEAN

Antarctic Circle

75°

Grassland   *Desert*   *Tundra*   *Barren*   *Urban*

World Population Density Map

This map shows which places in the world have many people and which have few people. The largest areas of dense population are in East Asia, South Asia, and Europe. Vast areas of the world are too cold, too dry, or too mountainous for dense population.

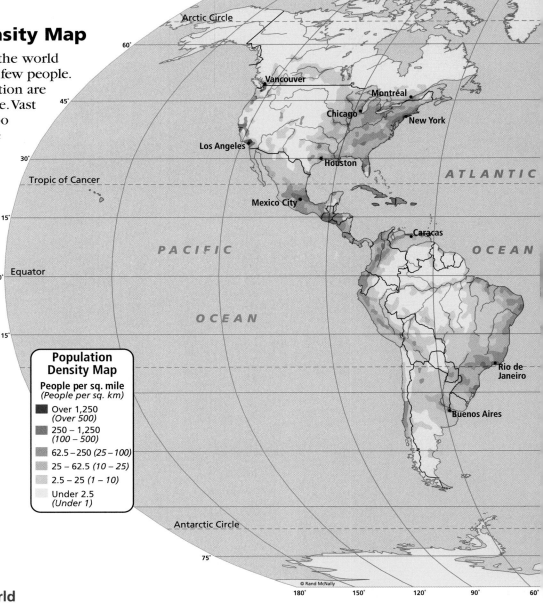

Population Density Map

People per sq. mile
(People per sq. km)

- Over 1,250 *(Over 500)*
- 250 – 1,250 *(100 – 500)*
- 62.5 – 250 *(25 – 100)*
- 25 – 62.5 *(10 – 25)*
- 2.5 – 25 *(1 – 10)*
- Under 2.5 *(Under 1)*

© Rand McNally

Children Around the World

North America

North America

Middle America

South America

Europe

World Population Growth

For most of human history, the world's population grew very slowly. About 250 years ago, it began to grow faster as people learned to control illnesses. Now people in many parts of the world are having smaller families, and the rate of growth may be slowing down.

ARCTIC OCEAN

Arctic Circle

Stockholm
Moscow
Yekaterinburg
London
Paris

Madrid
Rome
Algiers
Tehrān
Beijing
Tōkyō

Cairo
PACIFIC

Tropic of Cancer

Mumbai
(Bombay)
OCEAN

Bangkok

Lagos
Equator

Nairobi

Jakarta
INDIAN

OCEAN
Tropic of Capricorn

Johannesburg
Sydney
Melbourne

SOUTHERN   OCEAN

Antarctic Circle

Africa

Middle East

Asia

Asia

Australia

Year

1500
1600
1700
1800
1900
2000

0   1,000,000,000   2,000,000,000   3,000,000,000   4,000,000,000   5,000,000,000   6,000,000,000   7,000,000,000

Population

World Economies Map

This map shows how people around the world make a living. Each color on the map shows the most important economic activity for that area.

Look at the bright yellow area of Canada and the United States. According to the map legend, agriculture is the most important economy there. If you went to this area, you would see farm fields, orchards, and farm animals such as dairy cows and pigs. You probably would see grain elevators, feed stores, and other businesses that support farming. Of course, you would see banks, office buildings, stores, and factories, but not as many as you would see in the areas colored red.

According to the map legend, the most important economic activities in the red areas are manufacturing and commerce. Manufacturing is making goods. Automobiles, computers, clothing, and skateboards are examples of goods.

Commerce is the buying and selling of goods. Commerce also includes the buying and selling of services. Medical care, banking, education, and cable television are examples of service industries. In Canada, the United States, Europe, and Japan more people work in service industries than in manufacturing or agriculture. If you went to the areas shown in red, you would see a concentration of banks, office buildings, factories, and stores. Many of the world's largest manufacturing and commerce areas are shown on this map.

According to the map legend, hunting, forestry, and subsistence farming are the most important economic activities in the brown areas. In these areas you would find people working on small farms, growing food for themselves and their families. You would find people hunting and fishing to get food for themselves and their families.

Economies Map

- Little or no activity
- Nomadic herding
- Hunting, forestry, subsistence farming
- Forestry
- Agriculture
- Stock raising
- Manufacturing, commerce
- Fishing

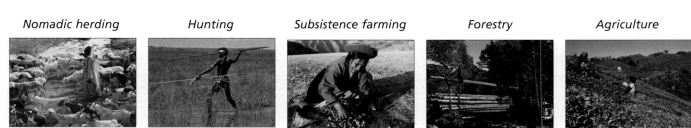

Nomadic herding   *Hunting*   *Subsistence farming*   *Forestry*   *Agriculture*

ARCTIC OCEAN

75°

Arctic Circle

60°

Stockholm

Moscow

45°

ndon

Paris

Beijing

30°

Madrid

Rome

Tōkyō

PACIFIC

Algiers

Tehrān

Cairo

Tropic of Cancer

OCEAN

Mumbai
(Bombay)

Bangkok

15°

Lagos

Equator 0°

Nairobi

15°

INDIAN

Jakarta

Tropic of Capricorn

OCEAN

30°

Johannesburg

Sydney

Melbourne

45°

60°

MERN   OCEAN

Antarctic Circle

75°

Agriculture   *Stock raising*   *Manufacturing*   *Commerce*   *Fishing*

World Fuel Deposits

Deposits of coal, petroleum, and natural gas are found in very limited parts of the world. The United States is fortunate to have significant deposits of all three.

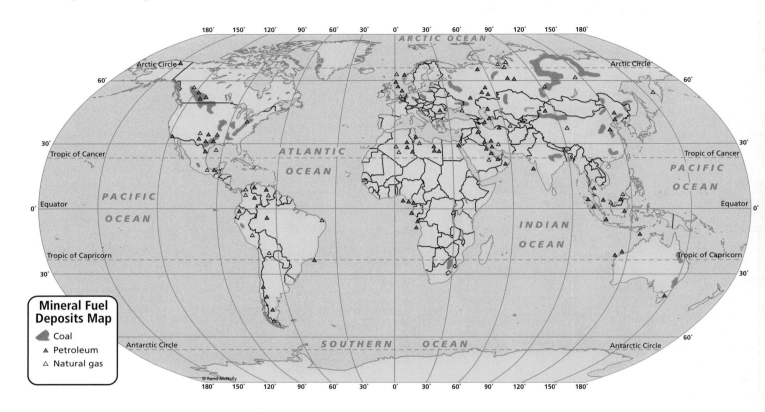

Mineral Fuel Deposits Map
- 🐾 Coal
- ▲ Petroleum
- △ Natural gas

© Rand McNally

World Coal Production
China and the United States, which have extensive deposits of coal, lead the world in coal production.

World Petroleum Production
Saudi Arabia, Russia, and the United States produce nearly one-third of the world's oil.

World Uranium Production
Canada and Australia lead the world in production of uranium, which is used as a fuel in nuclear energy plants.

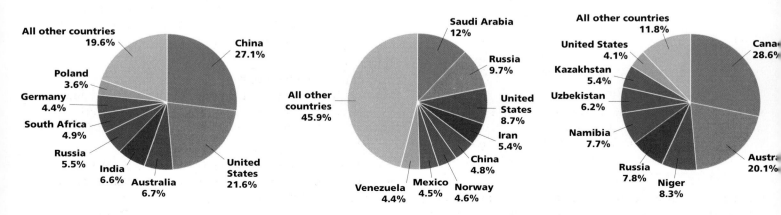

World Coal Production
- All other countries 19.6%
- China 27.1%
- United States 21.6%
- Australia 6.7%
- India 6.6%
- Russia 5.5%
- South Africa 4.9%
- Germany 4.4%
- Poland 3.6%

World Petroleum Production
- Saudi Arabia 12%
- Russia 9.7%
- United States 8.7%
- Iran 5.4%
- China 4.8%
- Norway 4.6%
- Mexico 4.5%
- Venezuela 4.4%
- All other countries 45.9%

World Uranium Production
- All other countries 11.8%
- United States 4.1%
- Kazakhstan 5.4%
- Uzbekistan 6.2%
- Namibia 7.7%
- Russia 7.8%
- Niger 8.3%
- Australia 20.1%
- Canada 28.6%

World Energy Consumption

Manufacturing, heating, and transportation are the three main ways that people use energy. This explains why the largest users of energy are industrialized countries that have large populations and relatively cold climates.

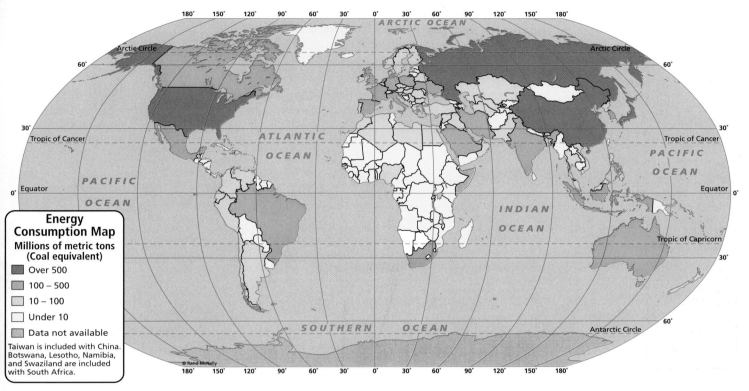

Energy
Consumption Map
Millions of metric tons
(Coal equivalent)
- Over 500
- 100 – 500
- 10 – 100
- Under 10
- Data not available

Taiwan is included with China. Botswana, Lesotho, Namibia, and Swaziland are included with South Africa.

Energy Terms

Coal:
A rock created from ancient plant life under enormous pressure. It is burned to produce heat and create steam for running machines or making electricity. Most coal, when burned, emits sulfur, a major component of acid rain.

Geothermal power:
Uses water heated naturally beneath the earth's surface. The steam that results powers engines that create electricity. Geothermal power is a clean source of energy, but it is available only in very limited areas.

Fossil fuels:
Created from remains of plants and animals over millions of years. Fossil fuels are not renewable sources of energy because it takes vast amounts of time to create them. Coal, oil, and natural gas are fossil fuels.

Hydroelectricity:
Generated by fast-moving water that is used to power generators. Dams on rivers provide sources of rapidly moving water. Hydroelectricity is a clean source of power, but the dams can have negative effects on their surroundings.

Natural gas:
A form of petroleum. A flammable gas used mainly as fuel for stoves, furnaces, and hot-water heaters. Natural gas is a clean-burning fuel.

Nuclear energy:
Created by splitting atoms. The energy is used to heat water that makes steam to drive electricity generators. The safety of nuclear plants and the hazardous wastes they create are of great concern.

Petroleum:
A liquid, also called oil. Petroleum is the most widely used source of energy in the world. It is used to produce gasoline, kerosene, and fuel oil. It is also used to manufacture plastics and other products.

Wind power and solar energy:
Two sources of renewable energy. They are not in wide use today, but in some places the use of wind to make electricity is increasing.

Plate Tectonics

Plate tectonics theory says that the earth's surface is divided into more than a dozen plates. These plates move very slowly, just a few inches a year. As they move, they collide or grind past each other. Most of the world's volcanoes and earthquakes occur at the places where plates meet.

Many plates collide with or grind past the Pacific Plate. The Ring of Fire is the name given to the band of earthquakes and volcanic activity around the Pacific Ocean.

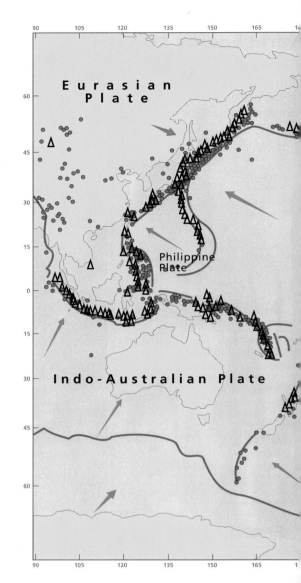

225 million years ago: Most of the world's land was together in a single "supercontinent." Scientists call this giant continent Pangaea.

180 million years ago: Pangaea split up into separate landmasses.

65 million years ago: The oceans as we know them today began to take shape. South America and India moved away from Africa.

The present day: India has joined with Asia, Australia has moved away from Antarctica, and North America has separated from Europe.

Some Notable Earthquakes

Year	Magnitude (Richter Scale)	Place	Estimated Deaths
2004	9.0	Sumatra, Indonesia	280,000 killed by earthquake and tsunami
1990	7.7	Iran	50,000 killed by earthquake and landslides
1976	7.5	Tangshan, China	255,000
1970	7.9	Peru	66,000
1964	9.2	Prince William Sound, AK	125 killed by earthquake and tsunami
1948	7.3	Turkmenistan	110,000
1927	7.9	Qinghai, China	200,000
1923	7.9	Japan	143,000 killed by earthquake and fire
1908	7.2	Italy	100,000 killed by earthquake and tsunami
1906	7.8	San Francisco, CA	3,000 killed by earthquake and fire

Damage from the 1906 San Francisco earthquake

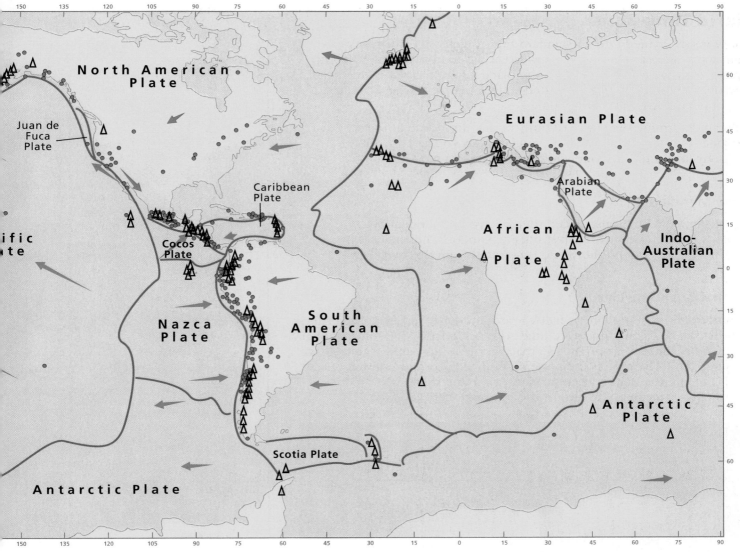

Antarctic Plate

Some Notable Volcanic Eruptions

Year	Magnitude Explosivity Index (VEI)	Name (location)	Estimated Deaths
1991	6	Mt. Pinatubo (Philippines)	350
1985	3	Nevado del Ruiz (Colombia)	25,000
1980	5	Mt. St. Helens (Washington, U.S.)	57
1963	3	Surtsey (Iceland)	Volcano creates new island
1902	4	Mt. Pelée (Martinique)	30,000
1883	6	Krakatoa (Indonesia)	36,000 killed, most by tsunami
1815	7	Gunung Tambora (Indonesia)	92,000
79	5	Vesuvius (Italy)	3,000 killed in Pompeii and Herculaneum

Eruption of Mt. St. Helens in 1980.

World Time Zones

The world is divided into 24 standard time zones. As Earth turns on its axis each day, the sun is overhead at different places at different times. Each time zone is based on the place where the sun is overhead at noon. The boundaries are adjusted so that people whose activities are connected live in the same time zone.

You can determine the standard time for any time zone in the world. Add one hour for each time zone you count as you go east. Subtract one hour for each time zone you count as you go west.

Prime Meridian

The Prime Meridian is also called the Greenwich Meridian because it passes through Greenwich, just outside London, England. It is 0° longitude. Time around the world is counted from this meridian.

International Date Line

The International Date Line is halfway around the world from the Prime Meridian, at 180° longitude. Like time zone boundaries, the International Date Line is adjusted from 180° so that people in the same country have the same day. The time is the same on both sides of the International Date Line, but the day is different. West of the International Date Line it is one day later than it is east of the International Date Line.

New Zealand, which lies just west of the International Date Line, is one of the first places in the world to greet each new day.

A strip of brass marks the Prime Meridian at the Royal Greenwich Observatory near London, England.

Examples of Time Changes

Auckland, New Zealand	Los Angeles, California, United States	Montréal, Québec, Canada	Rio de Janeiro, Brazil

*12 midnight
June 26*

*4 a.m.
June 25*

*7 a.m.
June 25*

*9 a.m.
June 25*

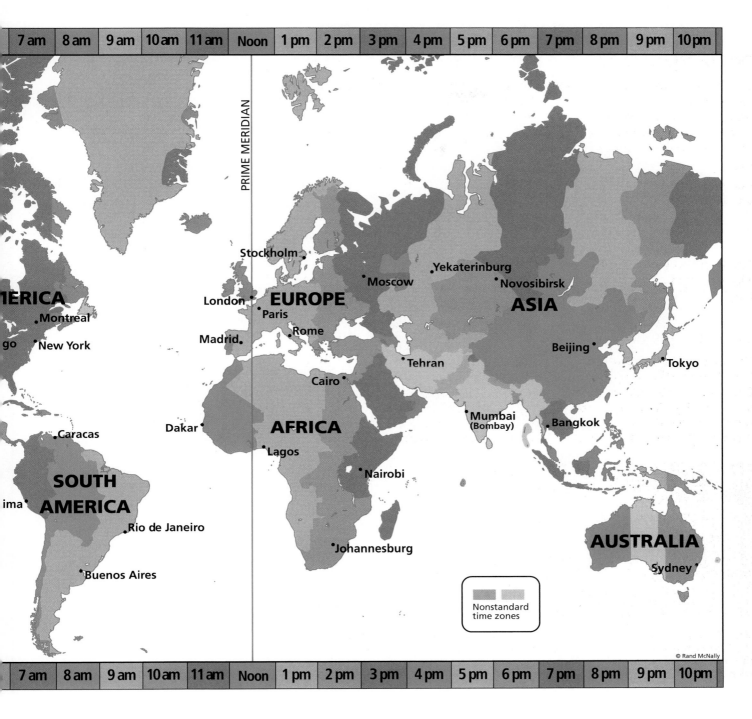

| 7 am | 8 am | 9 am | 10 am | 11 am | Noon | 1 pm | 2 pm | 3 pm | 4 pm | 5 pm | 6 pm | 7 pm | 8 pm | 9 pm | 10 pm |

PRIME MERIDIAN

Stockholm · Moscow · Yekaterinburg · Novosibirsk

London · EUROPE · ASIA
Paris ·
Rome ·
Madrid ·
Beijing · Tokyo ·

Tehran ·

Cairo ·

Dakar · AFRICA
Mumbai (Bombay) · Bangkok

Lagos ·

Nairobi ·

MERICA
Montreal ·
go · New York ·
Caracas ·

SOUTH AMERICA
ima ·
Rio de Janeiro

Buenos Aires ·

Johannesburg ·

AUSTRALIA
Sydney ·

Nonstandard time zones

© Rand McNally

| 7 am | 8 am | 9 am | 10 am | 11 am | Noon | 1 pm | 2 pm | 3 pm | 4 pm | 5 pm | 6 pm | 7 pm | 8 pm | 9 pm | 10 pm |

Paris, France

1 p.m.
June 25

Moscow, Russia

3 p.m.
June 25

Novosibirsk, Russia

6 p.m.
June 25

Tokyo, Japan

9 p.m.
June 25

North America

Mt. McKinley, Alaska, U.S.

North America is the third-largest continent. About 506,000,000 people live there.

It stretches 5,400 miles (8,700 kilometers) from northern Canada to the Panama-Colombia border.

Three countries—Canada, the United States, and Mexico—make up most of North America. The Caribbean island countries, the countries from Belize to Panama, and the island of Greenland make up the rest of the continent.

Central America is a region within North America. It is made up of the countries of Belize, Guatemala, Honduras, El Salvador, Nicaragua, Costa Rica, and Panama.

Central America is part of a larger region of North America called Middle America. This region consists of Central America, Mexico, and the Caribbean countries.

Generally, the people of North America have used its rich natural resources to great advantage. But not everyone has benefited. There are people throughout the continent who struggle with poverty, particularly in Central America and some Caribbean countries.

Parliament Hill, Ottawa, Ontario, Canada

San Francisco, California, U.S.

Pyramid of the Sun, Mexico

Did You Know?

Greenland, which is part of North America, is the largest island in the world.

A Historical Look At North America

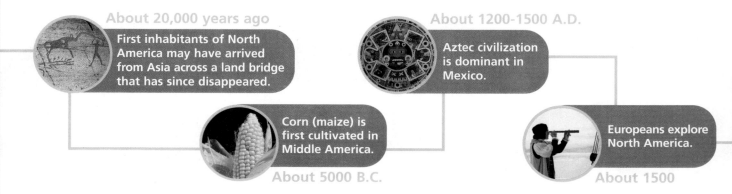

About 20,000 years ago
First inhabitants of North America may have arrived from Asia across a land bridge that has since disappeared.

About 1200-1500 A.D.
Aztec civilization is dominant in Mexico.

Corn (maize) is first cultivated in Middle America.
About 5000 B.C.

Europeans explore North America.
About 1500

Urbanization in North America

In the late nineteenth century and early twentieth century, many new factories were built in the United States and Canada. People moved from farms to cities to take jobs in factories and offices. They were joined by immigrants from many countries. After World War II, people in cities moved to suburbs, and cities began to grow together, especially along the East Coast between Boston and Washington, D.C. Now people in Mexico are moving to cities and to suburbs. Some of them cannot find steady jobs, and the cities have trouble providing water, sewers, and schools for the rapidly growing populations.

Rising Urban Population
Urban population as a percentage of total population, 1900–2000

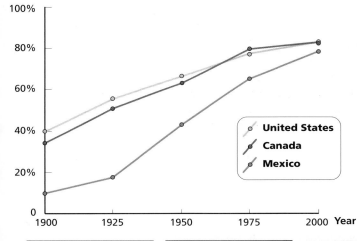

- United States
- Canada
- Mexico

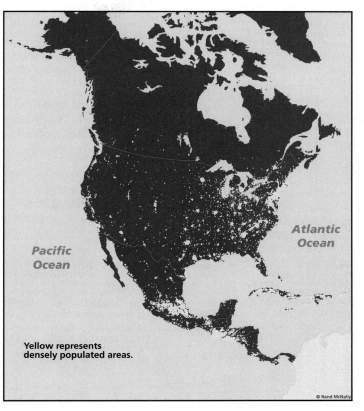

Pacific Ocean

Atlantic Ocean

Yellow represents densely populated areas.

© Rand McNally

New York City, the largest city in the United States

Abandoned farm on the Great Plains

Village scene in Mexico

Suburban sprawl in Colorado

Toronto, the largest city in Canada

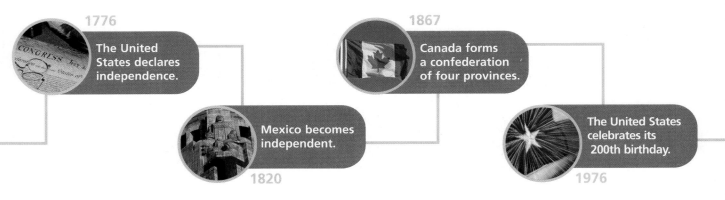

1776
The United States declares independence.

1820
Mexico becomes independent.

1867
Canada forms a confederation of four provinces.

1976
The United States celebrates its 200th birthday.

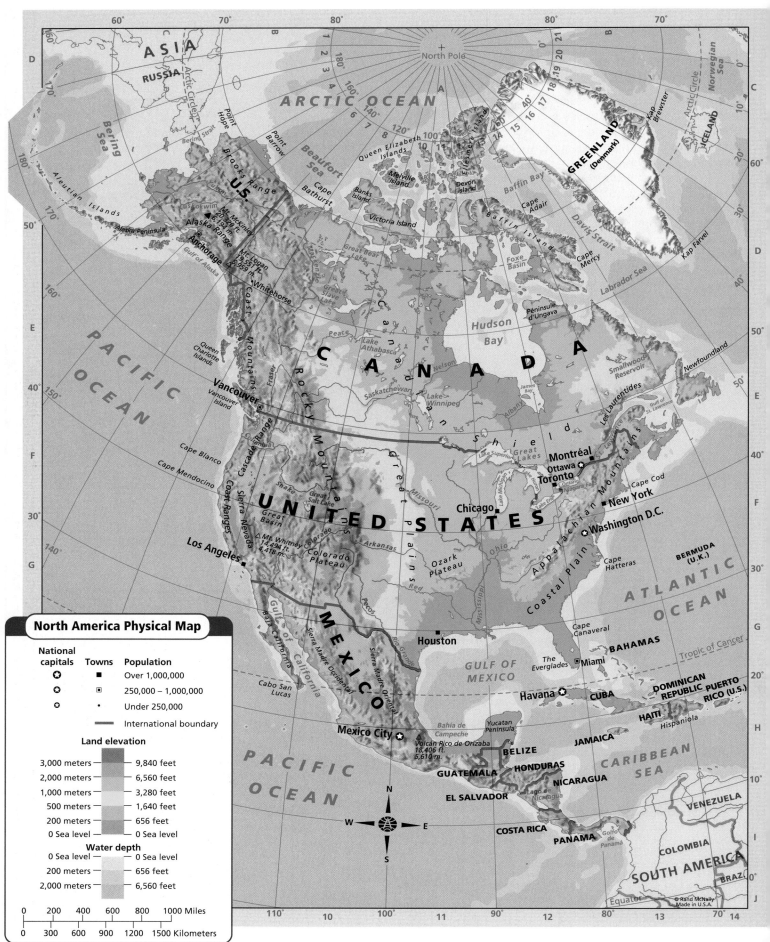

North America Physical Map

National capitals	Towns	Population
✪	■	Over 1,000,000
✪	▣	250,000 – 1,000,000
✪	•	Under 250,000
	⎯⎯	International boundary

Land elevation

3,000 meters	9,840 feet
2,000 meters	6,560 feet
1,000 meters	3,280 feet
500 meters	1,640 feet
200 meters	656 feet
0 Sea level	0 Sea level

Water depth

0 Sea level	0 Sea level
200 meters	656 feet
2,000 meters	6,560 feet

0 200 400 600 800 1000 Miles

0 300 600 900 1200 1500 Kilometers

ASIA
RUSSIA
Arctic Circle
Point Hope
Point Barrow
Bering Sea
Bering Strait
Aleutian Islands
Alaska Peninsula
Kuskokwim
Brooks Range
U.S.
Mt. McKinley 20,320 ft. 6,194 m.
Alaska Range
Anchorage
Mt. Logan 19,551 ft. 5,959 m.
Whitehorse
Gulf of Alaska
Coast Mountains

ARCTIC OCEAN
North Pole
Queen Elizabeth Islands
Ellesmere Island
Melville Island
Banks Island
Devon Island
Victoria Island
Cape Bathurst
Beaufort Sea
Mackenzie
Great Bear Lake
Great Slave Lake
Lake Athabasca
Peace
Nelson
Saskatchewan
Lake Winnipeg

GREENLAND (Denmark)
Kap Brewster
Arctic Circle
ICELAND
Norwegian Sea
Baffin Bay
Cape Adair
Baffin Island
Davis Strait
Cape Mercy
Labrador Sea
Kap Farvel
Foxe Basin
Hudson Bay
Péninsule d'Ungava

CANADA
Canadian Shield
James Bay
Smallwood Reservoir
Newfoundland
Les Laurentides
Gulf of St. Lawrence

PACIFIC OCEAN
Queen Charlotte Islands
Vancouver
Vancouver Island
Fraser
Columbia
Rocky Mountains
Great Plains
Lake Superior
Great Lakes
Lake Michigan
Lake Huron
Lake Erie
Lake Ontario
Niagara Falls
St. Lawrence
Montréal
Ottawa
Toronto
Appalachian Mountains
Cape Cod
New York
Washington D.C.

Cape Blanco
Cape Mendocino
Cascade Range
Columbia
Snake
Sierra Nevada
Coast Ranges
Great Salt Lake
Great Basin
UNITED STATES
Mt. Whitney 14,494 ft. 4,418 m.
Los Angeles
Colorado
Colorado Plateau
Arkansas
Missouri
Ozark Plateau
Ohio
Mississippi
Red
Chicago
Coastal Plain
Cape Hatteras
BERMUDA (U.K.)

Gulf of California
Baja California
Cabo San Lucas
Sierra Madre Occidental
Rio Grande
Pecos
MEXICO
Sierra Madre Oriental
Houston
Cape Canaveral
The Everglades
Miami
BAHAMAS
Tropic of Cancer
GULF OF MEXICO
Havana
CUBA
DOMINICAN REPUBLIC
PUERTO RICO (U.S.)
HAITI
Hispaniola

PACIFIC OCEAN
Mexico City
Bahía de Campeche
Yucatán Peninsula
Volcán Pico de Orizaba 18,406 ft. 5,610 m.
BELIZE
GUATEMALA
HONDURAS
JAMAICA
CARIBBEAN SEA
EL SALVADOR
NICARAGUA
Lago de Nicaragua
COSTA RICA
PANAMA
Golfo de Panamá
ATLANTIC OCEAN

N
W   E
S

VENEZUELA
COLOMBIA
SOUTH AMERICA
BRAZIL
Equator

© Rand McNally
Made in U.S.A.

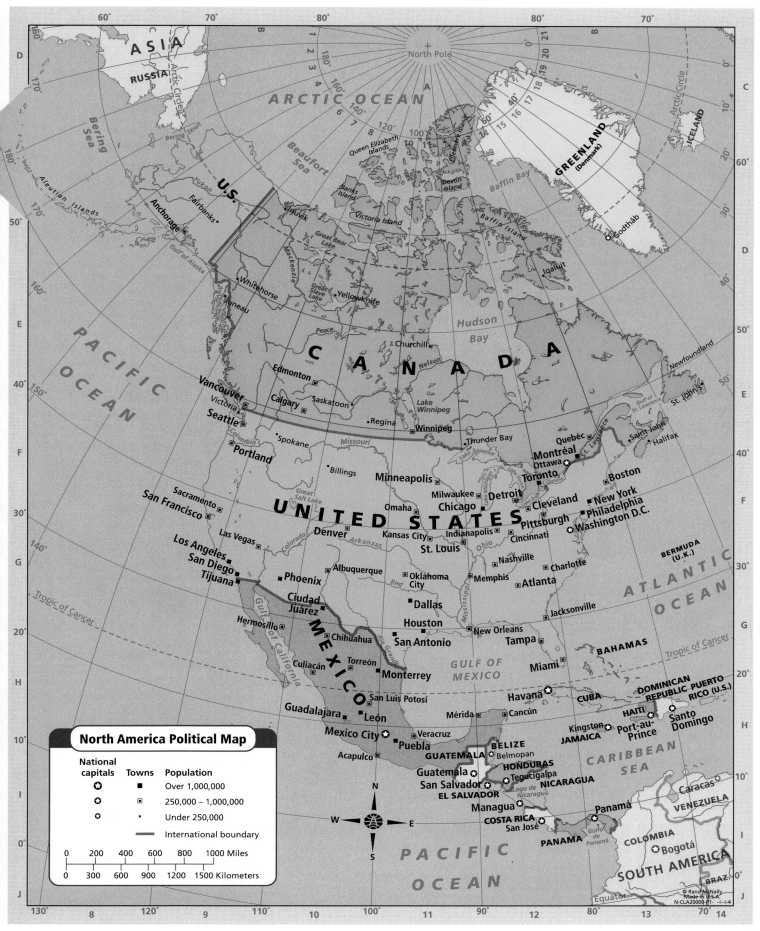

ASIA

RUSSIA

Bering Sea

Aleutian Islands

ARCTIC OCEAN

North Pole

Beaufort Sea

Queen Elizabeth Islands

Banks Island

Victoria Island

Devon Island

Ellesmere Island

Baffin Bay

GREENLAND (Denmark)

Godthåb

ICELAND

Baffin Island

Arctic Circle

PACIFIC OCEAN

U.S.

Anchorage

Fairbanks

Juneau

Inuvik

Whitehorse

Great Bear Lake

Mackenzie

Yellowknife

Great Slave Lake

Peace

Churchill

Hudson Bay

Iqaluit

Newfoundland

St. John's

C A N A D A

Edmonton

Calgary

Saskatoon

Regina

Lake Winnipeg

Winnipeg

Thunder Bay

Nelson

Gulf of St. Lawrence

Saint John

Halifax

Vancouver

Victoria

Seattle

Spokane

Portland

Missouri

Billings

Minneapolis

Milwaukee

Chicago

Detroit

Cleveland

Pittsburgh

Buffalo

Québec

Montréal

Ottawa

Toronto

Lake Superior

Lake Michigan

Lake Huron

Lake Erie

Lake Ontario

St. Lawrence

Boston

New York

Philadelphia

Washington D.C.

Sacramento

San Francisco

Las Vegas

Great Salt Lake

U N I T E D   S T A T E S

Denver

Colorado

Kansas City

Omaha

St. Louis

Indianapolis

Cincinnati

Ohio

Nashville

Charlotte

Los Angeles

San Diego

Tijuana

Phoenix

Albuquerque

Oklahoma City

Red

Memphis

Atlanta

ATLANTIC OCEAN

BERMUDA (U.K.)

Ciudad Juárez

Hermosillo

Chihuahua

M E X I C O

Culiacán

Torreón

Monterrey

San Luis Potosí

Dallas

Houston

San Antonio

Rio Grande

New Orleans

Mississippi

Tampa

Jacksonville

Miami

BAHAMAS

Tropic of Cancer

GULF OF MEXICO

Guadalajara

León

Mexico City

Puebla

Acapulco

Veracruz

Mérida

Cancún

Havana

CUBA

JAMAICA

Kingston

HAITI

Port-au-Prince

DOMINICAN REPUBLIC

PUERTO RICO (U.S.)

Santo Domingo

BELIZE

Belmopan

GUATEMALA

HONDURAS

Tegucigalpa

Guatemala

San Salvador

EL SALVADOR

Managua

NICARAGUA

Lago de Nicaragua

COSTA RICA

San José

PANAMA

Panamá

Golfo de Panamá

CARIBBEAN SEA

Caracas

VENEZUELA

COLOMBIA

Bogotá

SOUTH AMERICA

BRAZ.

Equator

PACIFIC OCEAN

Gulf of California

Gulf of Alaska

Yukon

Columbia

Arctic Circle

Tropic of Cancer

N W E S

North America Political Map

National capitals

⊛ Over 1,000,000

⊙ 250,000 – 1,000,000

⊙ Under 250,000

Towns

■ Over 1,000,000

▣ 250,000 – 1,000,000

• Under 250,000

Population

━━ International boundary

0 200 400 600 800 1000 Miles

0 300 600 900 1200 1500 Kilometers

© Rand McNally
Made in U.S.A.
N-CLA20000-P1- -4-4-4

Climate

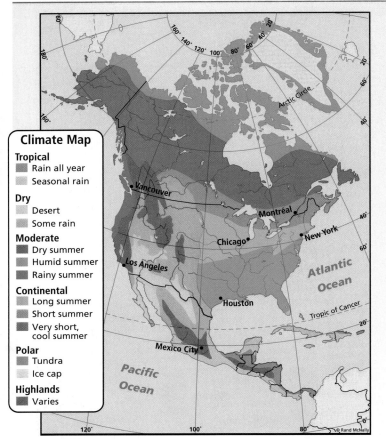

Climate Map

Tropical
- Rain all year
- Seasonal rain

Dry
- Desert
- Some rain

Moderate
- Dry summer
- Humid summer
- Rainy summer

Continental
- Long summer
- Short summer
- Very short, cool summer

Polar
- Tundra
- Ice cap

Highlands
- Varies

Environments

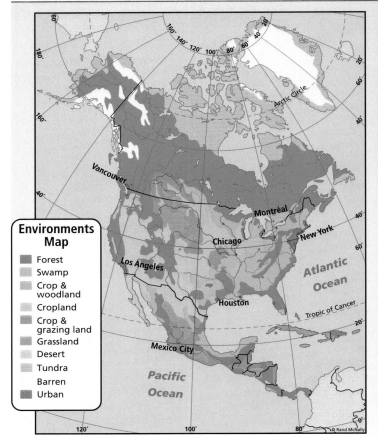

Environments Map
- Forest
- Swamp
- Crop & woodland
- Cropland
- Crop & grazing land
- Grassland
- Desert
- Tundra
- Barren
- Urban

Population

More than one-half of North Americans live in the United States. Canada is the continents's largest country in area, but it is home to only six percent of the continent's population.

All other countries 15%

Canada 6%

Mexico 21%

United States 58%

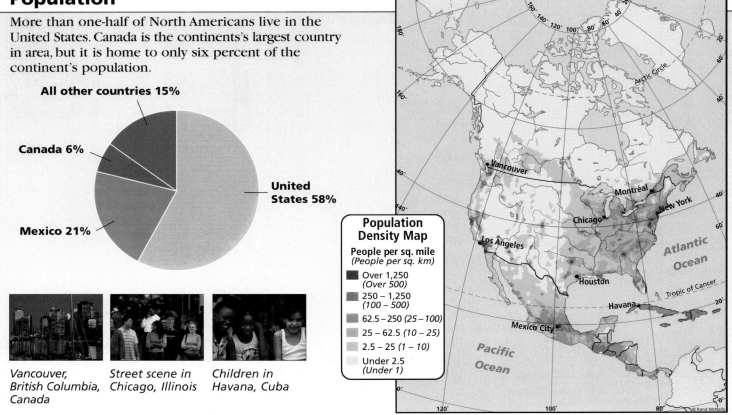

Vancouver, British Columbia, Canada

Street scene in Chicago, Illinois

Children in Havana, Cuba

Population Density Map

People per sq. mile
(People per sq. km)
- Over 1,250 *(Over 500)*
- 250 – 1,250 *(100 – 500)*
- 62.5 – 250 *(25 – 100)*
- 25 – 62.5 *(10 – 25)*
- 2.5 – 25 *(1 – 10)*
- Under 2.5 *(Under 1)*

The Great Lakes

The Great Lakes lie on the border between the United States and Canada. Canals allow ocean-going ships to travel to the lakes and between them. Together, the lakes and canals form a huge waterway that connects cities far inland in the United States and Canada with the ocean.

Size rank	Lake	Area sq. miles / sq. kilometers	Greatest depth feet / meters
1	Superior	31,700 / 82,100	1,332 / 406
2	Huron	23,000 / 59,600	750 / 229
3	Michigan	22,300 / 57,800	925 / 282
4	Erie	9,910 / 25,700	210 / 64
5	Ontario	7,340 / 18,960	802 / 244

Pictured Rocks cliffs are on Lake Superior, the largest of the Great Lakes.

The Welland Canal in Ontario, Canada, connects Lake Erie and Lake Ontario.

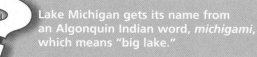

Did You Know?

Lake Michigan gets its name from an Algonquin Indian word, *michigami*, which means "big lake."

Relative Depths of the Great Lakes

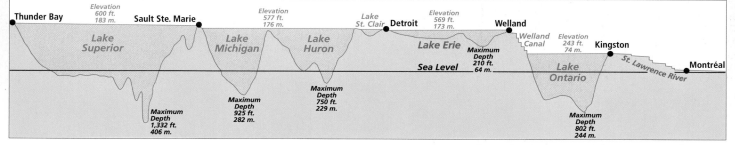

Economies

The map at right shows that agriculture is the most important economy for a large part of North America. Much of the continent's manufacturing and commerce is concentrated in a wide band between Chicago and New York.

In 1994, Canada, the United States, and Mexico enacted the North American Free Trade Agreement (NAFTA) to remove all trade restrictions between the three countries.

Fishing trawlers in California

Grain elevators in Alberta, Canada

Factory worker in Mexico

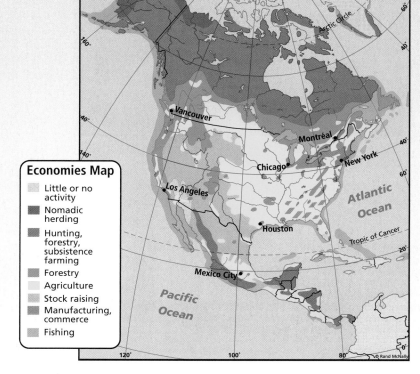

Economies Map

- Little or no activity
- Nomadic herding
- Hunting, forestry, subsistence farming
- Forestry
- Agriculture
- Stock raising
- Manufacturing, commerce
- Fishing

Natural Hazards

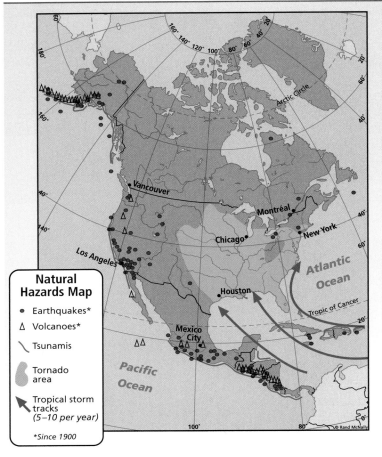

Natural Hazards Map
- Earthquakes*
- △ Volcanoes*
- \ Tsunamis
- Tornado area
- Tropical storm tracks (5–10 per year)

*Since 1900

This satellite image shows a hurricane approaching the Atlantic coast of Florida.

Twister!
Tornadoes are rapidly rotating columns of air. They are usually funnel-shaped, and their winds may reach 200–500 miles per hour (320–800 kilometers per hour). They are usually less than one-quarter mile (400 meters) wide but are extremely destructive. Texas has more tornadoes than any other state. Oklahoma ranks second in number of tornadoes, and Kansas ranks third.

What If?

? Scientists track hurricanes by radar and satellites. What could happen if there were no way to warn people about these tropical storms?

Transportation

Automobiles in Mexico City add to the severe pollution problem there.

Automobiles per 1,000 people
More people in rich countries—especially those countries that do not offer much public transportation—own cars.

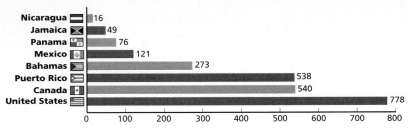

Nicaragua	16
Jamaica	49
Panama	76
Mexico	121
Bahamas	273
Puerto Rico	538
Canada	540
United States	778

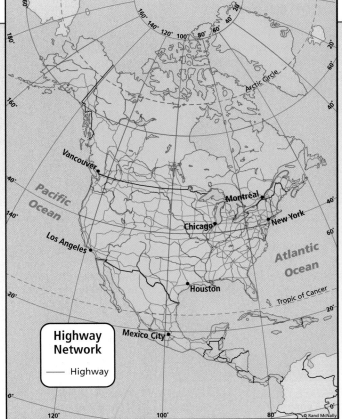

Highway Network
— Highway

Energy

Most nuclear power plants in North America are in the eastern and central United States.

The Hoover Dam in Nevada provides hydroelectric power to three states.

Wind power is a promising alternative energy source.

Electricity Production by Type

More than two-thirds of North America's electricity is produced by power plants that burn coal, oil, and natural gas. This is called thermal energy. Most of the remaining electricity comes from nuclear plants and hydroelectric, or waterpower, plants. Less than one percent of the continent's electricity is produced by geothermal plants, which tap into the heat of the Earth's molten interior.

Geothermal 1%
Hydro 14%
Nuclear 16%
Thermal 69%

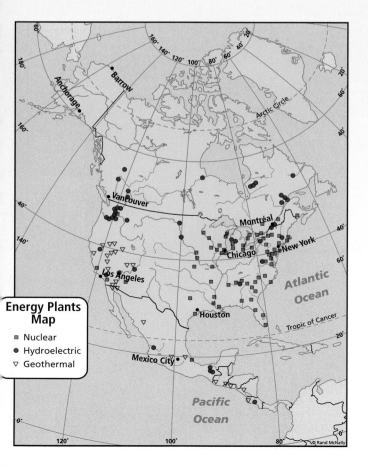

Energy Plants Map
- ■ Nuclear
- ● Hydroelectric
- ▽ Geothermal

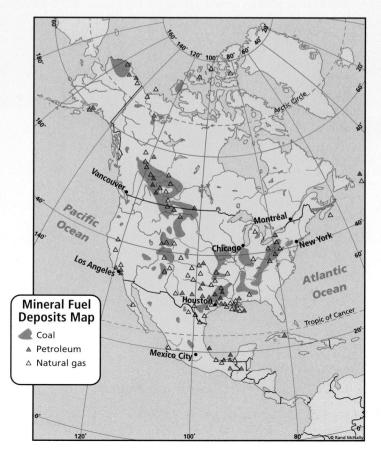

Mineral Fuel Deposits Map
- Coal
- ▲ Petroleum
- △ Natural gas

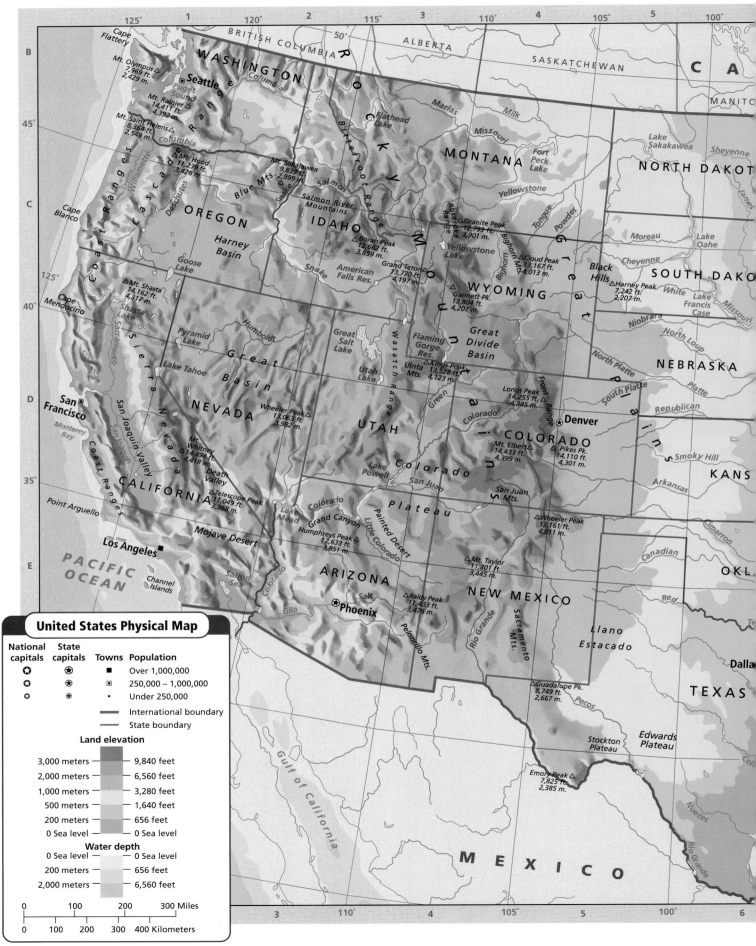

United States Physical Map

National capitals	State capitals	Towns	Population
⊙	★	■	Over 1,000,000
⊙	★	▣	250,000 – 1,000,000
⊛	✷	•	Under 250,000

━━━ International boundary
─── State boundary

Land elevation

3,000 meters	9,840 feet
2,000 meters	6,560 feet
1,000 meters	3,280 feet
500 meters	1,640 feet
200 meters	656 feet
0 Sea level	0 Sea level

Water depth

0 Sea level	0 Sea level
200 meters	656 feet
2,000 meters	6,560 feet

0   100   200   300 Miles

0 100 200 300 400 Kilometers

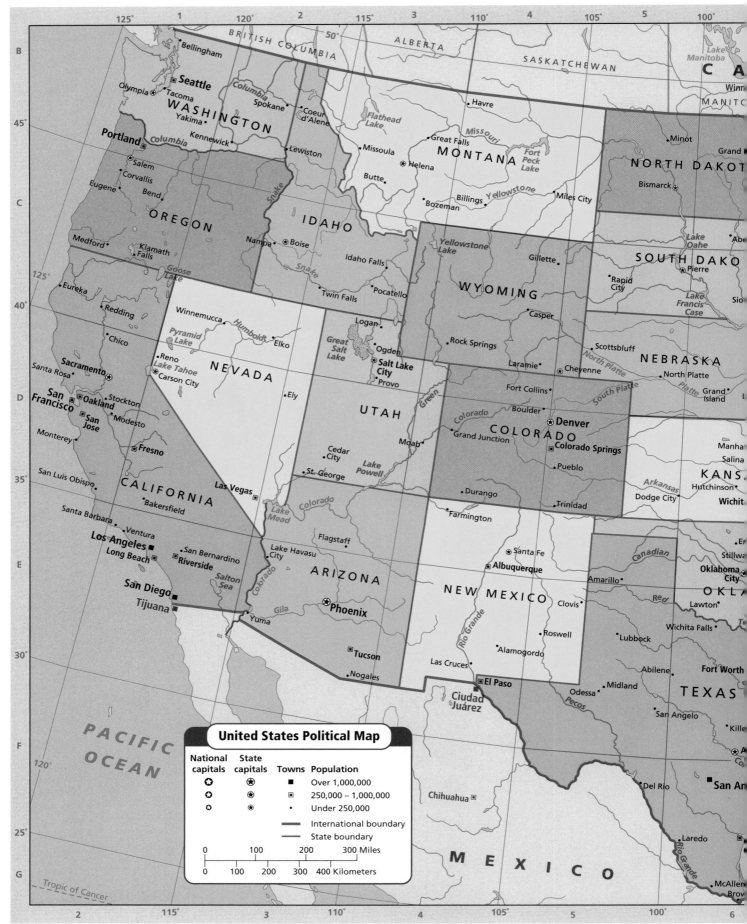

United States Political Map

National capitals	State capitals	Towns	Population
✪	✪	■	Over 1,000,000
✪	✪	▣	250,000 – 1,000,000
✪	✪	•	Under 250,000
			International boundary
			State boundary

0   100   200   300 Miles

0   100   200   300   400 Kilometers

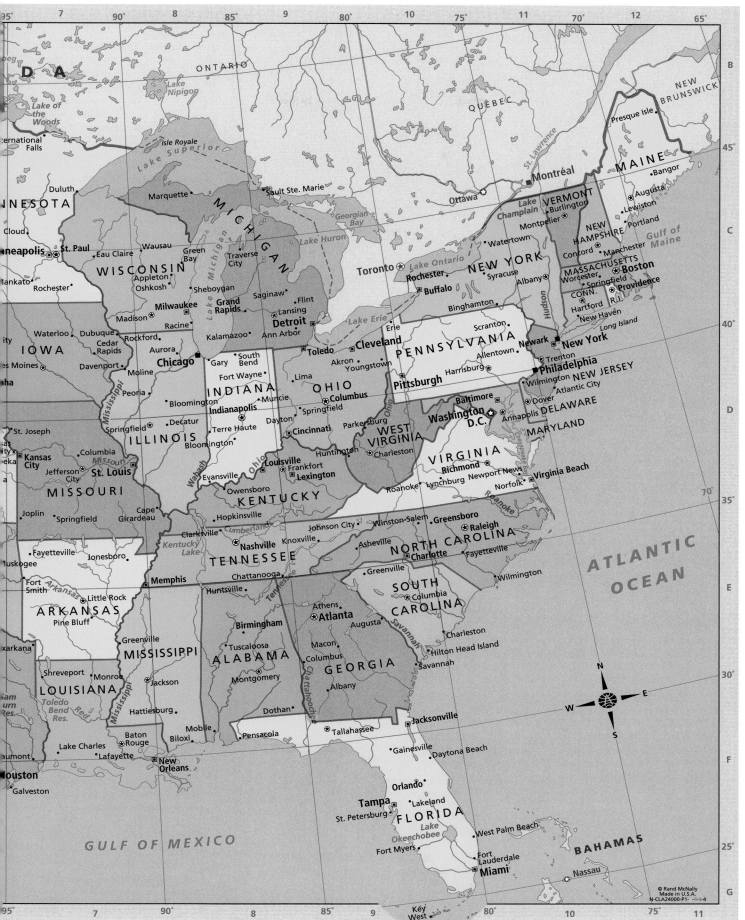

DA
ONTARIO

Lake of the Woods
Lake Nipigon
Isle Royale
Lake Superior

NEW BRUNSWICK

QUÉBEC

St. Lawrence
Presque Isle

International Falls

MAINE
Bangor

Duluth
Marquette
MICHIGAN
Sault Ste. Marie
Georgian Bay
Ottawa
Montréal
Lake Champlain
VERMONT
Burlington
Augusta
Lewiston
Portland

NNESOTA

Lake Huron
NEW HAMPSHIRE
Montpelier
Gulf of Maine

Cloud
Wausau
Green Bay
Traverse City

Watertown
NEW YORK
Concord
Manchester

neapolis
St. Paul
Eau Claire
WISCONSIN
Appleton
Oshkosh
Sheboygan

Toronto
Lake Ontario
Rochester
Syracuse
Albany
MASSACHUSETTS
Worcester
Springfield
Boston

lankato
Rochester
Milwaukee
Grand Rapids
Saginaw
Flint

Buffalo
Binghamton
Hudson
Hartford
CONN.
New Haven
Providence
R.I.

Madison
Racine
Lansing
Detroit
Lake Erie
Erie
Scranton
PENNSYLVANIA
Allentown
Long Island

Waterloo
Dubuque
Rockford
Kalamazoo
Ann Arbor
Toledo
Cleveland
Akron
Youngstown
Harrisburg
Newark
New York

IOWA
Cedar Rapids
Aurora
Chicago
Gary
South Bend
Lima
OHIO
Pittsburgh
Trenton
Philadelphia
Wilmington
NEW JERSEY
Atlantic City

es Moines
Davenport
Moline
Fort Wayne
INDIANA
Muncie
Columbus
Springfield
Dover
DELAWARE

maha
Peoria
Bloomington
Indianapolis
Dayton
Cincinnati
Parkersburg
Baltimore
Washington D.C.
Annapolis
MARYLAND

St. Joseph
Decatur
Springfield
Terre Haute
Bloomington
ILLINOIS
Huntington
WEST VIRGINIA
Charleston

at
Columbia
Missouri
Louisville
Frankfort
Lexington
Ohio
VIRGINIA
Richmond

Kansas City
eka
Jefferson City
St. Louis
Evansville
Wabash
Roanoke
Lynchburg
Newport News
Norfolk
Virginia Beach

MISSOURI
Owensboro
KENTUCKY
Hopkinsville
Roanoke

Joplin
Springfield
Cape Girardeau
Clarksville
Cumberland
Johnson City
Winston-Salem
Greensboro
Raleigh

Fayetteville
Jonesboro
Kentucky Lake
Nashville
Knoxville
Asheville
NORTH CAROLINA
Fayetteville

Muskogee
ARKANSAS
Clarksville
TENNESSEE
Chattanooga
Charlotte

Fort Smith
Arkansas
Little Rock
Memphis
Huntsville
Tennessee
Greenville
SOUTH CAROLINA
Columbia
Wilmington

xarkana
Pine Bluff
Birmingham
Athens
Atlanta
Augusta
Savannah
Charleston

Greenville
Tuscaloosa
Macon
Columbus
Hilton Head Island

MISSISSIPPI
ALABAMA
GEORGIA
Savannah

Shreveport
Monroe
Jackson
Montgomery
Albany
Chattahoochee

LOUISIANA
Toledo Bend Res.
Red
Hattiesburg
Dothan
Tallahassee
Jacksonville

Sam urn Res.
Baton Rouge
Mobile
Biloxi
Pensacola

Lake Charles
Lafayette
New Orleans
Gainesville
Daytona Beach

eaumont
Houston
Galveston
Orlando
Lakeland
West Palm Beach

Tampa
St. Petersburg
FLORIDA
Lake Okeechobee
Fort Lauderdale

GULF OF MEXICO
Fort Myers
Miami
BAHAMAS
Nassau

ATLANTIC OCEAN

N
W E
S

Key West

B

C

D

E

F

G

45°

40°

35°

30°

25°

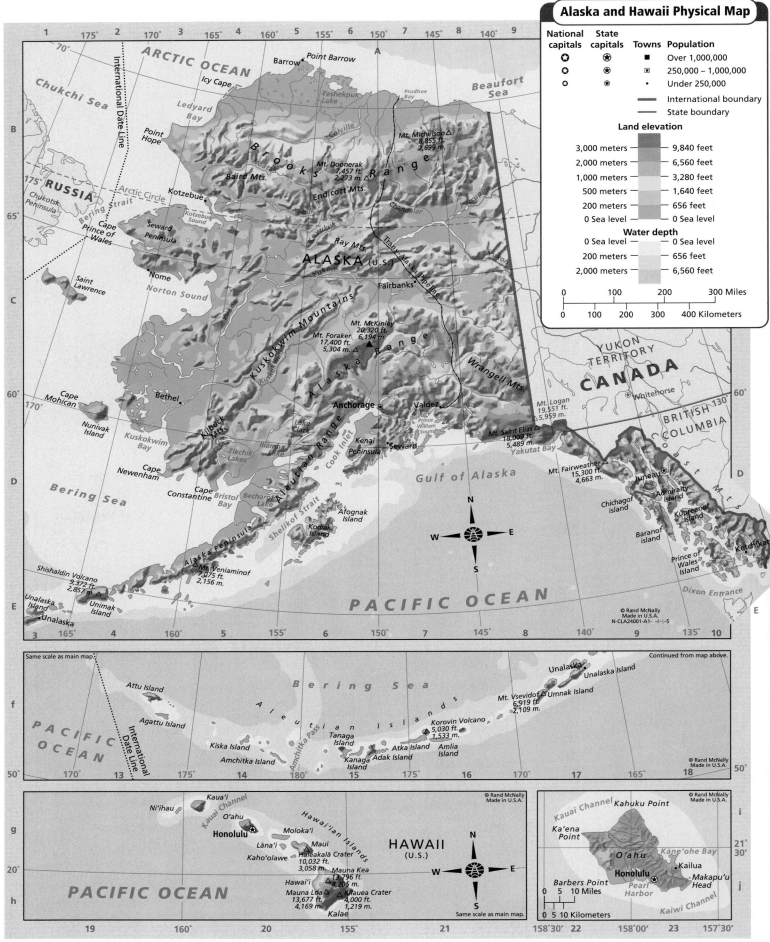

Alaska and Hawaii Physical Map

National capitals	State capitals	Towns	Population
⊛	⊛	■	Over 1,000,000
⊙	⊛	⊡	250,000 – 1,000,000
○	⊛	•	Under 250,000

International boundary
State boundary

Land elevation

3,000 meters	9,840 feet
2,000 meters	6,560 feet
1,000 meters	3,280 feet
500 meters	1,640 feet
200 meters	656 feet
0 Sea level	0 Sea level

Water depth

0 Sea level	0 Sea level
200 meters	656 feet
2,000 meters	6,560 feet

0   100   200   300 Miles
0 100 200 300 400 Kilometers

© Rand McNally
Made in U.S.A.
N-CLA24001-A1- -4-5-5

Location of Alaska and Hawaii

The states of Alaska and Hawaii are separated from the 48 conterminous states. Canada lies between Alaska and the other states. Hawaii is a chain of islands in the Pacific Ocean.

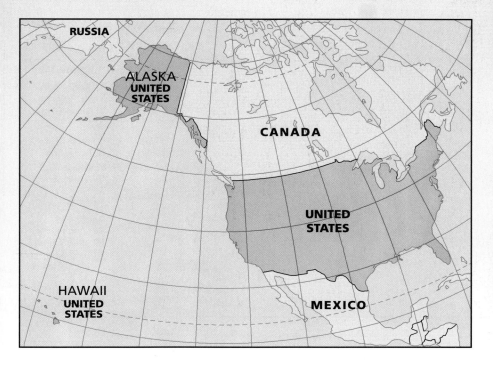

The United States annexed Hawaii in 1898. It became the 50th state in 1959. Here, waves crash along the coast of Maui.

The United States purchased Alaska from Russia in 1867. Alaska became the 49th state in 1959. This is Anchorage, the state's largest city.

Indian Reservations of the Conterminous United States

About two million Native Americans, or American Indians, live in the United States. Half of them live on or near reservations.

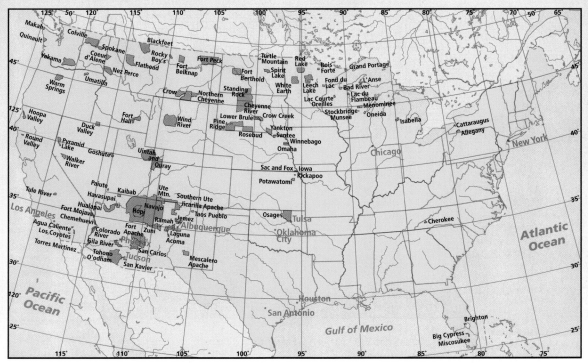

Pueblo Indian ruins in New Mexico reflect an ancient culture.

Flathead Indian Reservation in Montana.

Sioux powwow dancer in full costume.

Climate

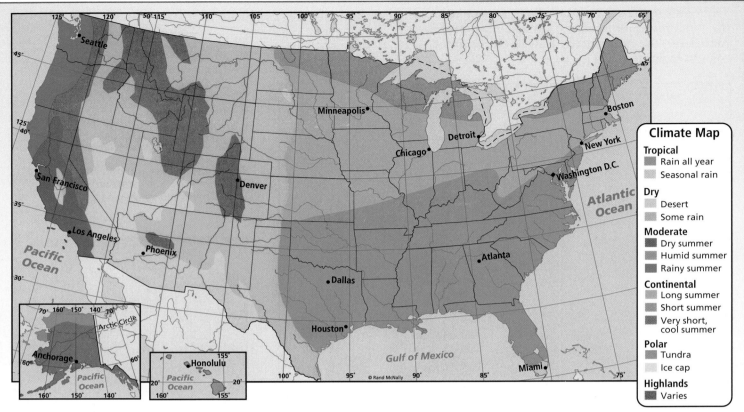

Climate Map

Tropical
- Rain all year
- Seasonal rain

Dry
- Desert
- Some rain

Moderate
- Dry summer
- Humid summer
- Rainy summer

Continental
- Long summer
- Short summer
- Very short, cool summer

Polar
- Tundra
- Ice cap

Highlands
- Varies

Economies

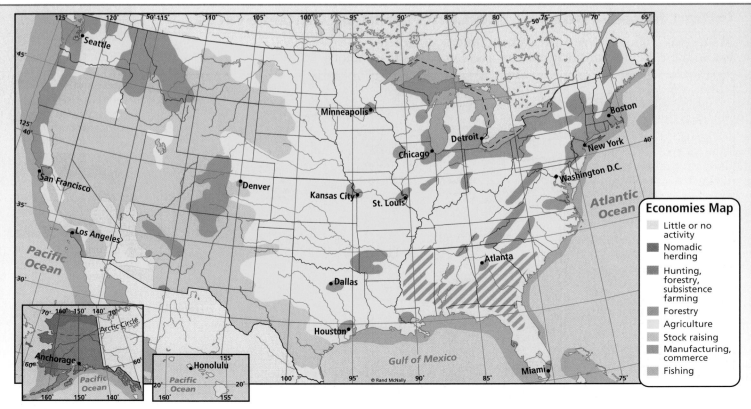

Economies Map
- Little or no activity
- Nomadic herding
- Hunting, forestry, subsistence farming
- Forestry
- Agriculture
- Stock raising
- Manufacturing, commerce
- Fishing

Population

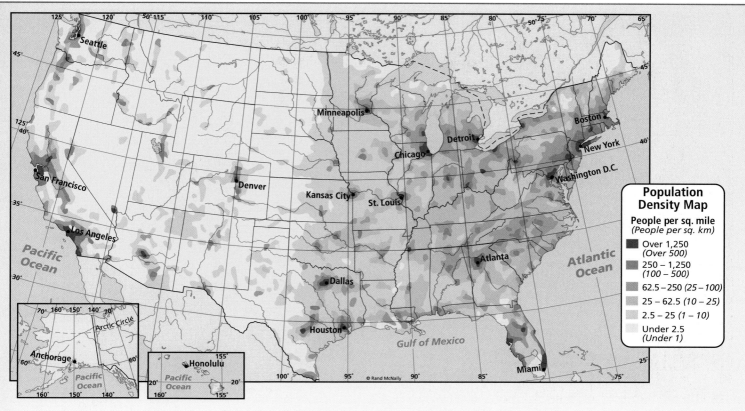

© Rand McNally

Population Density Map

People per sq. mile
(People per sq. km)

- Over 1,250 (Over 500)
- 250 – 1,250 (100 – 500)
- 62.5 – 250 (25 – 100)
- 25 – 62.5 (10 – 25)
- 2.5 – 25 (1 – 10)
- Under 2.5 (Under 1)

The United States has always been a nation of immigrants. It is one of the most culturally diverse countries in the world.

More than three-fourths of all Americans live in cities and towns.

Urban and Rural Population in the United States

1920

Rural 49% Urban 51%

2000

Rural 21% Urban 79%

City Landmarks

Many cities have famous landmarks, such as buildings, bridges, and monuments. How many of these landmarks, and their cities, can you name? The answers are at the bottom of the page.

1   **2**   **3**   **4**   **5**   **6**

Answers: 1. The Gateway Arch in St. Louis, Missouri. 2. The Space Needle in Seattle, Washington. 3. The Alamo in San Antonio, Texas. 4. The Golden Gate Bridge in San Francisco, California. 5. The Empire State Building in New York, New York. 6. The Corn Palace in Mitchell, South Dakota.

Environments

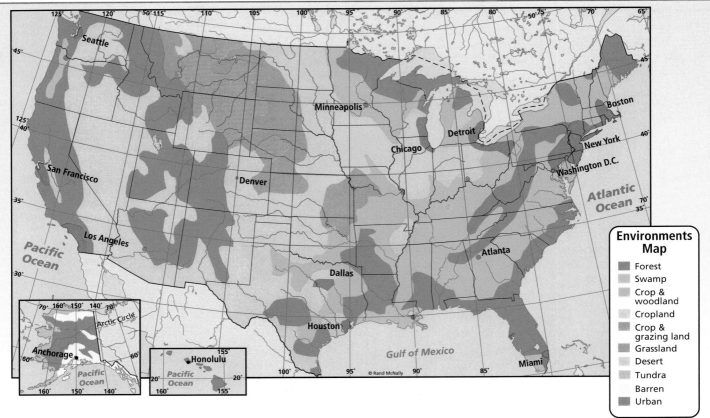

Environments Map

- Forest
- Swamp
- Crop & woodland
- Cropland
- Crop & grazing land
- Grassland
- Desert
- Tundra
- Barren
- Urban

Transportation

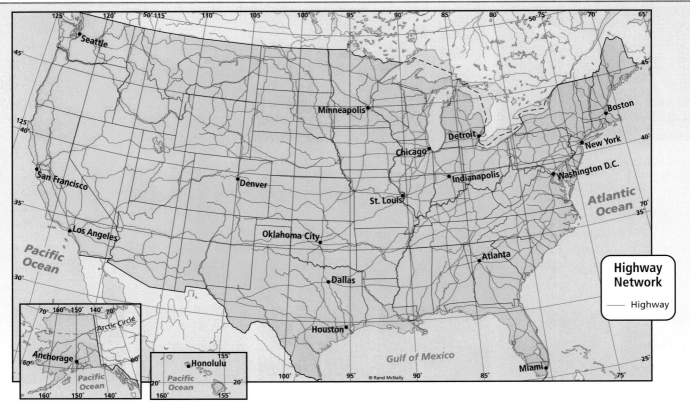

Highway Network

— Highway

United States Regions

The United States can be divided into regions in many different ways. On Map 1, states in the conterminous United States are divided into regions according to their geographical location. Alaska and Hawaii are not included in a region on this map.

On Map 2, all 50 states belong to a region. Some regions are named for a physical feature they share, such as the Rocky Mountains. Some regions are named for their location in the United States, such as the Southwest.

There are many opinions about what to call the different regions. There are also many opinions about where the boundary lines belong. What do you call the region where you live? Why?

The pages that follow show information about the regions shown on Map 2.

The Northeast

The Northeast originally was settled by people from Western Europe. In fact, the six states east of New York are known as New England. The Northeast was the site of five of the original 13 colonies. Because much of the land is not suitable for farming, manufacturing has always been important in this region.

Vermont is known for its brilliant fall colors and its abundant dairy farms.

A lighthouse on the Maine coast is a reminder of New England's seafaring days.

States of the Northeast

State	Land Area (square miles)	Population	Capital
Connecticut	4,845	3,503,600	Hartford
Maine	30,862	1,317,300	Augusta
Massachusetts	7,840	6,416,500	Boston
New Hampshire	8,968	1,299,500	Concord
New York	47,214	19,227,100	Albany
Rhode Island	1,045	1,080,600	Providence
Vermont	9,250	621,400	Montpelier

New York, New York, is the largest city in the Northeast and in the United States.

The original Mayflower brought 102 passengers from England to Massachusetts in 1620. Today, visitors can tour this replica in Plymouth, Massachusetts.

Niagara Falls, in New York and Canada, provides hydroelectric power to the Northeast.

The Mid-Atlantic

The Mid-Atlantic region is small in size, but heavily populated. Oil, steel, and coal from this region fueled America's industry and power for many decades. Washington, D.C., the national capital, is here, but it is not in any state. The letters "D.C." stand for District of Columbia, a federal district that is 61 square miles in area.

The Senate and House of Representatives meet in the U.S. Capitol Building in Washington, D.C.

Gettysburg National Military Park in Gettysburg, Pennsylvania, is a memorial to soldiers of the Civil War.

States of the Mid-Atlantic

State	Land Area (square miles)	Population	Capital
Delaware	1,954	830,400	Dover
Maryland	9,774	5,558,100	Annapolis
New Jersey	7,417	8,698,900	Trenton
Pennsylvania	44,817	12,406,300	Harrisburg
West Virginia	24,078	1,815,400	Charleston
Washington, D.C.*	61	553,500	--

* Washington, D.C., is not a state but a federal district.

Philadelphia, Pennsylvania, ranks as the largest city in the Mid-Atlantic region.

Atlantic City, Cape May, and other resort cities draw millions of visitors to the New Jersey shore each year.

West Virginia is the most rural state in the Mid-Atlantic region. This restored grist mill is located in Babcock State Park.

The South

The warm, humid climate of the South creates ideal conditions for growing cotton, sugarcane, and rice. The South is now also an important manufacturing region. Tourism, particularly in Florida, brings millions of dollars to the region.

The Great Smoky Mountains in Tennessee and North Carolina are part of the Appalachian mountain chain.

The space shuttle is launched at Cape Canaveral, Florida.

States of the South

State	Land Area (square miles)	Population	Capital
Alabama	50,744	4,530,200	Montgomery
Arkansas	52,068	2,752,600	Little Rock
Florida	53,927	17,397,200	Tallahassee
Georgia	57,906	8,829,400	Atlanta
Kentucky	39,728	4,092,891	Frankfort
Louisiana	43,562	4,145,900	Baton Rouge
Mississippi	46,907	2,903,000	Jackson
North Carolina	48,711	8,541,200	Raleigh
South Carolina	30,109	4,198,100	Columbia
Tennessee	41,217	5,901,000	Nashville
Virginia	39,594	7,459,800	Richmond

Miami Beach, Florida, is a popular vacation spot.

Swamps and bayous cover much of southern Louisiana.

Charleston, South Carolina, is noted for its architecture.

Nashville, the capital of Tennessee, is known as Music City, U.S.A.

The Mississippi River is one of the nation's most important waterways.

The Midwest

The Midwest has some of the most fertile soil for farming in the world. Large manufacturing cities such as Cleveland, Detroit, and Chicago have grown up along the shores of the Great Lakes.

Much of the land in Wisconsin is used for agriculture.

Chicago, Illinois, is the third-largest city in the United States.

States of the Midwest

State	Land Area (square miles)	Population	Capital
Illinois	55,584	12,713,600	Springfield
Indiana	35,867	6,237,600	Indianapolis
Iowa	55,869	2,954,500	Des Moines
Michigan	56,804	10,112,600	Lansing
Minnesota	79,610	5,101,000	St. Paul
Missouri	68,886	5,754,600	Jefferson City
Ohio	40,948	11,459,000	Columbus
Wisconsin	54,310	5,509,000	Madison

Sunflowers grow on fertile prairie land in southeastern Minnesota.

The Mississippi River flows past downtown St. Louis and the graceful Gateway Arch.

Corn is the most important crop in the Midwest.

The Great Plains

Although the Great Plains are flat, they are high in elevation. This elevation increases steadily from east to west. Look at the physical map of the United States to see the elevation change. The Great Plains states are major producers of wheat and beef cattle.

Scotts Bluff in Nebraska was an important landmark for pioneers heading west on the California and Oregon trails.

Cropland covers much of Kansas.

States of the Great Plains

State	Land Area (square miles)	Population	Capital
Kansas	81,815	2,735,500	Topeka
Nebraska	76,872	1,747,200	Lincoln
North Dakota	68,976	634,400	Bismarck
South Dakota	75,885	770,900	Pierre

Circular fields are a sign of center-pivot irrigation systems, which tap into underground water.

Abandoned farms are a common sight on the Great Plains. Many areas have been losing population for decades.

In the Badlands of South Dakota, wind and water have sculpted the land into fantastic shapes.

The Southwest

Many people have moved to the Southwest in recent decades because of its warm, sunny climate. Texas, the largest and most populous state in the region, has over 22 million people. Lack of water has become a problem as the population continues to grow.

Dallas is the second-largest city in Texas. The urban area has a population of more than five million.

Monument Valley in Arizona and Utah provides an example of a dry Southwest landscape.

States of the Southwest

State	Land Area (square miles)	Population	Capital
Arizona	113,635	5,743,800	Phoenix
New Mexico	121,356	1,903,300	Santa Fe
Oklahoma	68,667	3,523,600	Oklahoma City
Texas	261,797	22,490,000	Austin

Plants cling to gypsum sand dunes in New Mexico's White Sands National Monument.

The Grand Canyon in Arizona was carved by the Colorado River over the course of millions of years.

Taos Pueblo in northern New Mexico has been inhabited for more than a thousand years.

The Rocky Mountains

Until recent decades, the Rocky Mountains region had very little population. The rugged mountains made it difficult for settlers to travel into the area. Now that modern transportation has made travel easier, the population is growing rapidly. Denver, Colorado, is a hub for the region.

The Grand Teton Mountains in Wyoming are among the youngest mountains in the United States.

Rock formations called "hoodoos" rise majestically in Utah's Bryce Canyon National Park.

States of the Rocky Mountains

State	Land Area (square miles)	Population	Capital
Colorado	103,718	4,601,400	Denver
Idaho	82,747	1,393,300	Boise
Montana	145,552	926,900	Helena
Nevada	109,826	2,334,800	Carson City
Utah	82,144	2,389,000	Salt Lake City
Wyoming	97,100	506,500	Cheyenne

The Las Vegas "strip" lights up the desert sky in southern Nevada.

The Cliff Palace in Mesa Verde National Park, Colorado, was built by Native Americans more than 700 years ago.

Ice-chiseled peaks soar skyward in Montana's Glacier National Park.

The Pacific

The Pacific states vary greatly in climate, population, and environment. The physical and thematic maps of the United States can help you see the differences. Farming has always been important, but the region also is a leader in communications and technology.

A flower farm thrives in the wet, cool climate of Washington's Olympic Peninsula.

Thanks to its balmy climate and breathtaking scenery, Hawaii enjoys a booming tourism industry.

States of the Pacific

State	Land Area (square miles)	Population	Capital	
Alaska	571,951	655,400	Juneau	
California	155,959	35,893,800	Sacramento	
Hawaii	6,423	1,262,800	Honolulu	
Oregon	95,997	3,594,600	Salem	
Washington	66,544	6,203,800	Olympia	

Much of Alaska is pristine wilderness.

Seattle, Washington, is a technology center. It is also an important trading partner with Pacific Rim nations.

Oregon's Crater Lake lies in the crater of a dormant volcano.

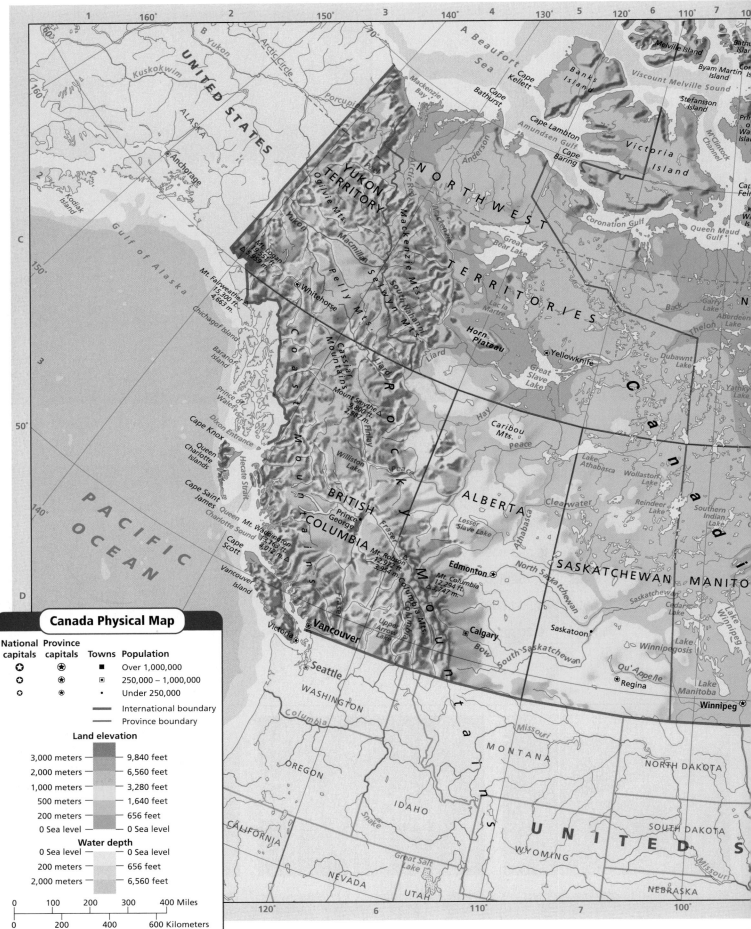

Canada Physical Map

National capitals	Province capitals	Towns	Population
✪	✪	■	Over 1,000,000
✪	✪	▣	250,000 – 1,000,000
✪	✪	•	Under 250,000

International boundary
Province boundary

Land elevation

3,000 meters	9,840 feet
2,000 meters	6,560 feet
1,000 meters	3,280 feet
500 meters	1,640 feet
200 meters	656 feet
0 Sea level	0 Sea level

Water depth

0 Sea level	0 Sea level
200 meters	656 feet
2,000 meters	6,560 feet

| 0 | 100 | 200 | 300 | 400 Miles |
| 0 | 200 | 400 | 600 Kilometers |

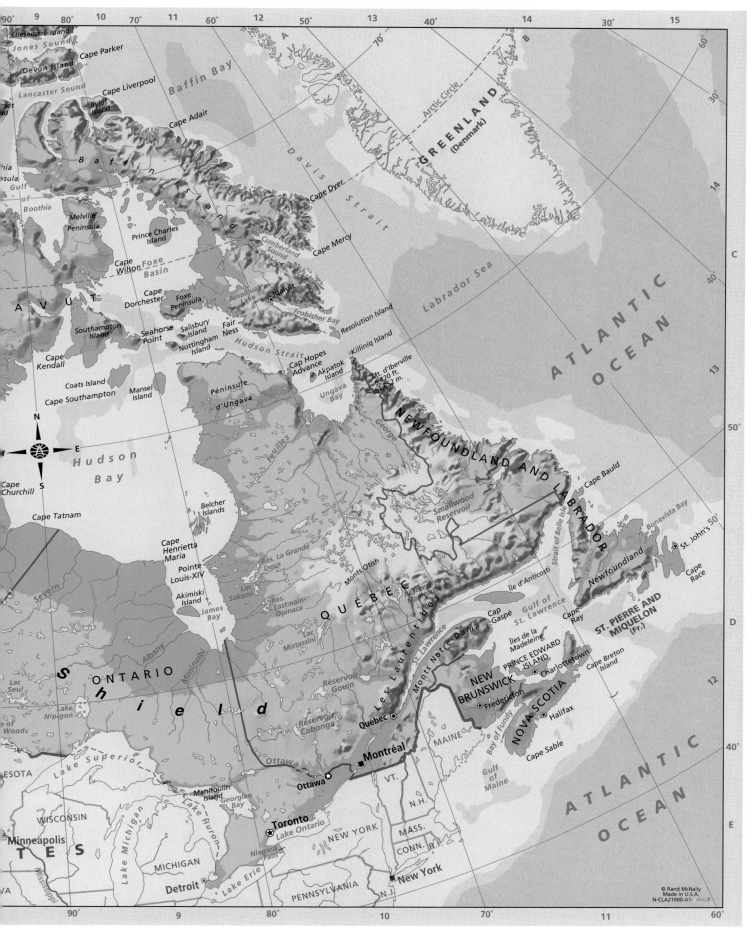

90° 9 80° 10 70° 11 60° 12 50° 13 40° 14 30° 15

Ellesmere Island
Jones Sound
Devon Island — Cape Parker
Cape Liverpool
Lancaster Sound
Bylot Island
Cape Adair
Baffin Bay

GREENLAND
(Denmark)
Arctic Circle

Davis Strait
Cape Dyer

Baffin Island

...hia
...sula
Gulf of Boothia
Melville Peninsula
Prince Charles Island
Cape Wilson
Foxe Basin
Cape Dorchester
Foxe Peninsula
Amadjuak Lake
Iqaluit
Cumberland Sound
Cape Mercy

Labrador Sea

ATLANTIC OCEAN

N A V U T
Southampton Island
Cape Kendall
Seahorse Point
Salisbury Island
Nottingham Island
Fair Ness
Frobisher Bay
Resolution Island
Hudson Strait
Cap Hopes Advance
Killiniq Island
Akpatok Island

Coats Island
Cape Southampton
Mansel Island
Péninsule d'Ungava
Ungava Bay
George
Mt. d'Iberville 5,420 ft. 1,652 m.

NEWFOUNDLAND AND LABRADOR

Cape Churchill
Cape Tatnam
Feuilles
Hudson Bay
Belcher Islands
Smallwood Reservoir
Cape Bauld

N E W S

Cape Henrietta Maria
Pointe Louis-XIV
Rés. La Grande Deux
Lac Sakami
Monts Otish
Réservoir Manicouagan
Bonavista Bay
St. John's 50°

Severn
Akimiski Island
James Bay
Rés. Eastmain-Opinaca
Lac Mistassini
QUÉBEC
Newfoundland
Cape Race

S h i e l d
ONTARIO
Albany
Missinaibi
Réservoir Gouin
Les Laurentides
Monts Notre-Dame
Île d'Anticosti
Gulf of St. Lawrence
Cap Ray
St. Lawrence
ST. PIERRE AND MIQUELON (Fr.)
Cape Breton Island

Lac Seul
Lake Nipigon
Réservoir Cabonga
Cap Gaspé
Îles de la Madeleine
PRINCE EDWARD ISLAND
Charlottetown
NEW BRUNSWICK
Fredericton
NOVA SCOTIA
Halifax

...of Woods
ESOTA
Lake Superior
Ottawa
Québec
Montréal
MAINE
Bay of Fundy
Cape Sable
Gulf of Maine

MINNESOTA
Manitoulin Island
Georgian Bay
Ottawa
VT.
N.H.

WISCONSIN
Lake Michigan
Lake Huron
Toronto
Lake Ontario
NEW YORK
MASS.
CONN. R.I.

Minneapolis
...TES
MICHIGAN
Niagara Falls
Lake Erie
Detroit
PENNSYLVANIA
N.J.
New York

ATLANTIC OCEAN

90° 9 80° 10 70° 11 60°

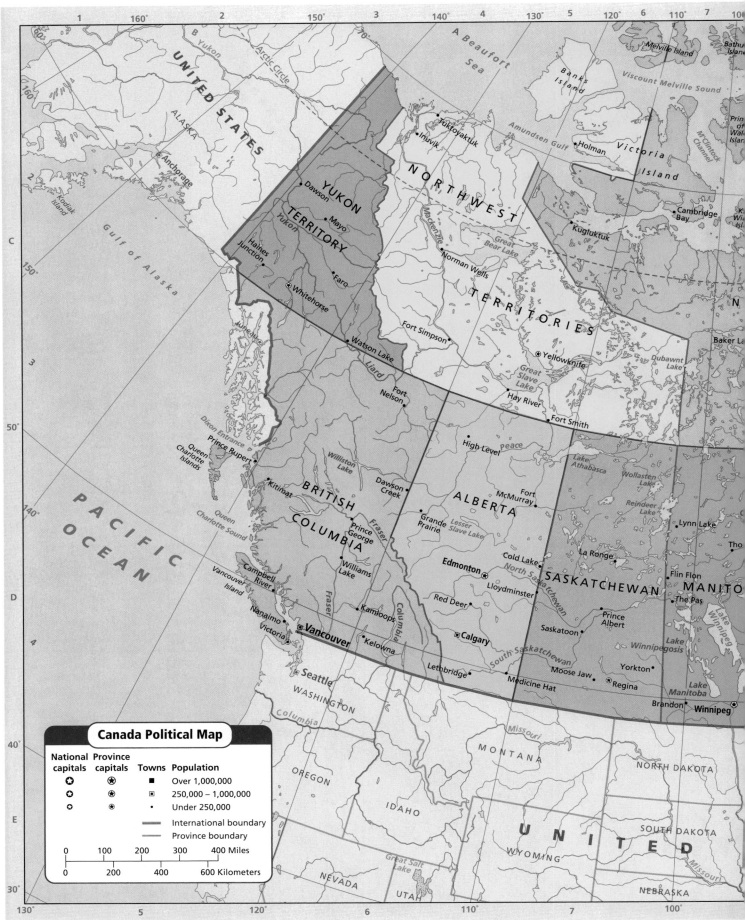

UNITED STATES

ALASKA

Yukon

Arctic Circle

B

A Beaufort Sea

Banks Island

Melville Island

Bathu Isla

Viscount Melville Sound

Prin of Wal Islan

M'Clintock Channel

Amundsen Gulf

•Holman

Victoria Island

•Tuktoyaktuk

•Inuvik

Anchorage•

Kodiak Island

Gulf of Alaska

YUKON TERRITORY

•Dawson

Yukon

•Mayo

NORTHWEST

Mackenzie

Great Bear Lake

•Norman Wells

Kugluktuk•

•Cambridge Bay

K Wi Isl

Haines Junction•

Faro•

✠Whitehorse

TERRITORIES

Juneau

Watson Lake•

Liard

Fort Simpson•

✠Yellowknife

Great Slave Lake

Baker La

N

Dixon Entrance

Prince Rupert•

Queen Charlotte Islands

Fort Nelson•

Hay River•

Fort Smith•

Dubawnt Lake

50°

Williston Lake

High Level•

Peace

Lake Athabasca

Wollaston Lake

PACIFIC OCEAN

Kitimat•

BRITISH COLUMBIA

Dawson Creek•

ALBERTA

Fort McMurray•

Reindeer Lake

Lynn Lake•

Tho

140°

Queen Charlotte Sound

Fraser

Prince George•

Grande Prairie•

Lesser Slave Lake

La Ronge•

SASKATCHEWAN

Flin Flon•

MANITO

Campbell River•

Williams Lake•

Cold Lake•

North Saskatchewan

The Pas•

Vancouver Island

Fraser

Nanaimo•

Victoria✠

Columbia

Kamloops•

Edmonton✪

Lloydminster•

Red Deer•

Saskatoon•

Prince Albert•

Lake Winnipegosis

Lake Winnipeg

⊡Vancouver

•Kelowna

⊡Calgary

South Saskatchewan

Moose Jaw•

Yorkton•

•Seattle

Lethbridge•

Medicine Hat•

✠Regina

Lake Manitoba

WASHINGTON

Columbia

Brandon•

Winnipeg✪

40°

Canada Political Map

National capitals	Province capitals	Towns	Population
✪	✪	■	Over 1,000,000
✪	✪	⊡	250,000 – 1,000,000
✪	✪	•	Under 250,000

───── International boundary

───── Province boundary

0   100   200   300   400 Miles

0   200   400   600 Kilometers

MONTANA

NORTH DAKOTA

OREGON

IDAHO

UNITED

SOUTH DAKOTA

NEVADA

WYOMING

Great Salt Lake

UTAH

Missouri

NEBRASKA

30°

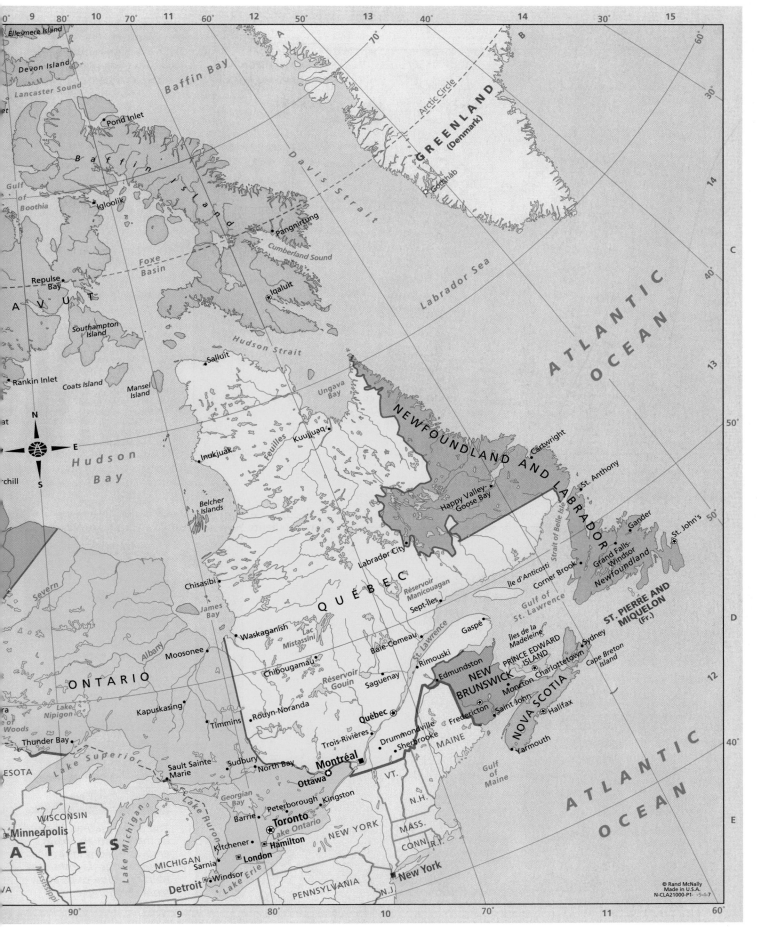

90° 9 80° 10 70° 11 60° 12 50° 13 40° 14 30° 15 60°

Ellesmere Island
Devon Island
Lancaster Sound
Baffin Bay

Pond Inlet

Baffin Island

GREENLAND
(Denmark)

Arctic Circle

Godthåb

Gulf of Boothia
Igloolik

Foxe Basin

Cumberland Sound
Pangnirtung

Davis Strait

Labrador Sea

ATLANTIC
OCEAN

A V U T
Repulse Bay

Iqaluit

Southampton Island

Rankin Inlet
Coats Island
Mansel Island

Hudson Strait

Salluit

Ungava Bay

NEWFOUNDLAND AND LABRADOR

Cartwright

N
W—E
S

Hudson Bay

Kuujjuaq
Feuilles

St. Anthony

Inukjuak

Happy Valley-Goose Bay

Belcher Islands

Strait of Belle Isle

James Bay

Chisasibi

QUÉBEC

Réservoir Manicouagan

Labrador City

Gander
St. John's

Grand Falls-Windsor
Newfoundland

Corner Brook
Île d'Anticosti

Severn

Sept-Îles

Gulf of St. Lawrence

ST. PIERRE AND MIQUELON (Fr.)

D

Waskaganish
Lac Mistassini

Albany

Moosonee

St. Lawrence

Baie-Comeau

Gaspé

Îles de la Madeleine

Sydney
Cape Breton Island

ONTARIO

Chibougamau
Réservoir Gouin

Rimouski

PRINCE EDWARD ISLAND

Moncton Charlottetown

Saguenay

Edmundston

NEW BRUNSWICK

12

Kapuskasing

Rouyn-Noranda

Fredericton

Saint John

NOVA SCOTIA

Lake Nipigon

Timmins

Québec

MAINE
Halifax

of Woods

Trois-Rivières

Drummondville
Sherbrooke

Yarmouth

Thunder Bay

Lake Superior

Sault Sainte Marie

Sudbury

North Bay

Montréal

VT.

Gulf of Maine

ATLANTIC

ESOTA

Ottawa

N.H.

OCEAN

Georgian Bay

Peterborough

Kingston

WISCONSIN

Barrie

Toronto

NEW YORK

MASS.

E

Minneapolis

Lake Ontario

CONN. R.I.

A T E S

Kitchener
Hamilton

Lake Michigan

MICHIGAN

London
Sarnia

Lake Huron

Windsor

New York

Detroit
Lake Erie

PENNSYLVANIA
N.J.

Mississippi

VA

© Rand McNally
Made in U.S.A.
N-CLA21000-P1- -5-4-7

90° 9 80° 10 70° 11 60°

Population

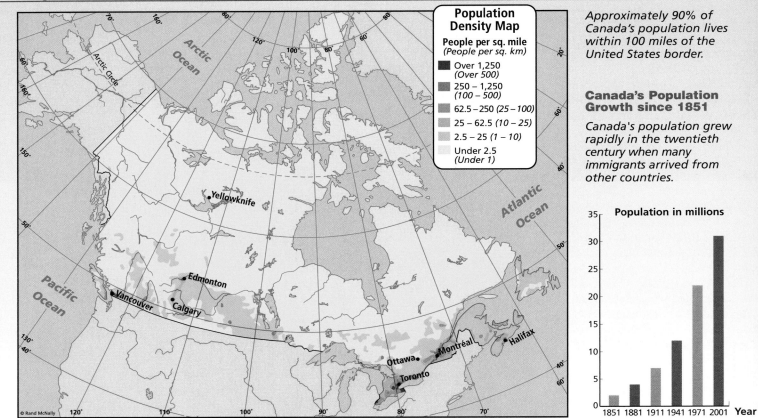

Population Density Map

People per sq. mile
(People per sq. km)

Over 1,250
(Over 500)

250 – 1,250
(100 – 500)

62.5 – 250 (25 – 100)

25 – 62.5 (10 – 25)

2.5 – 25 (1 – 10)

Under 2.5
(Under 1)

Approximately 90% of Canada's population lives within 100 miles of the United States border.

Canada's Population Growth since 1851

Canada's population grew rapidly in the twentieth century when many immigrants arrived from other countries.

Population in millions

Year	1851	1881	1911	1941	1971	2001

Environments

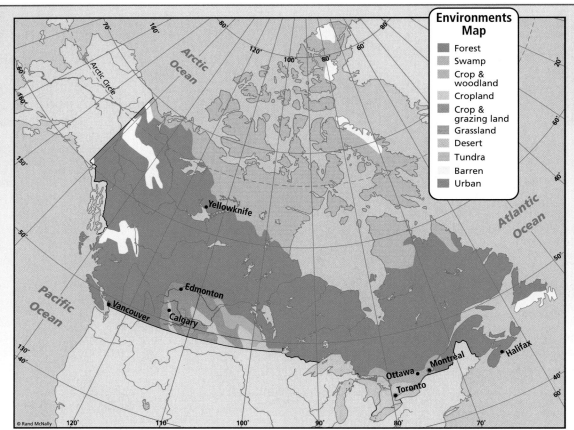

Environments Map

Forest
Swamp
Crop & woodland
Cropland
Crop & grazing land
Grassland
Desert
Tundra
Barren
Urban

The Canadian Rocky Mountains extend through Alberta, British Columbia, and the Yukon Territory.

The rocky plateau known as the Canadian Shield ends as headlands at the water's edge. Lighthouses help to guide ships away from the danger.

Transportation

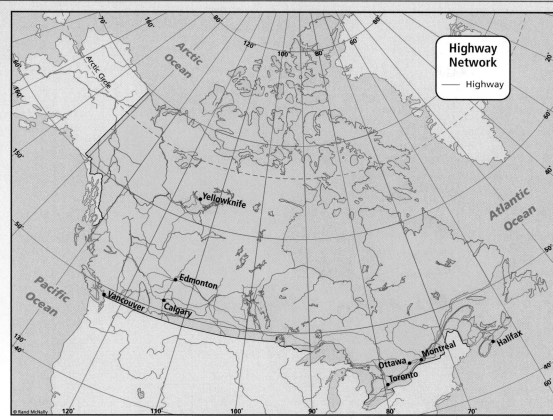

Highway Network
— Highway

Scenic roads wind along the coasts of Canada's Maritime Provinces.

Canada's highways help to connect widely separated clusters of people across the country's vast expanse.

Economies

Most of Canada's grain is grown in the "prairie provinces" of Alberta, Saskatchewan, and Manitoba.

Atlantic coast fishing is important to Canada's economy.

Toronto is Canada's financial center and the headquarters for many of the country's largest companies.

Canada's Economy

Services—such as banking, transportation, and government—account for more than two-thirds of Canada's economic output.

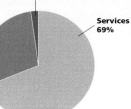

Agriculture 2%
Services 69%
Industry 29%

World Lumber Exports

Canada, with its vast forestlands, accounts for nearly one-third of the world's lumber exports.

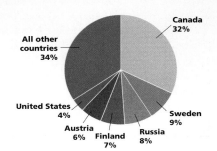

Canada 32%
All other countries 34%
United States 4%
Austria 6%
Finland 7%
Russia 8%
Sweden 9%

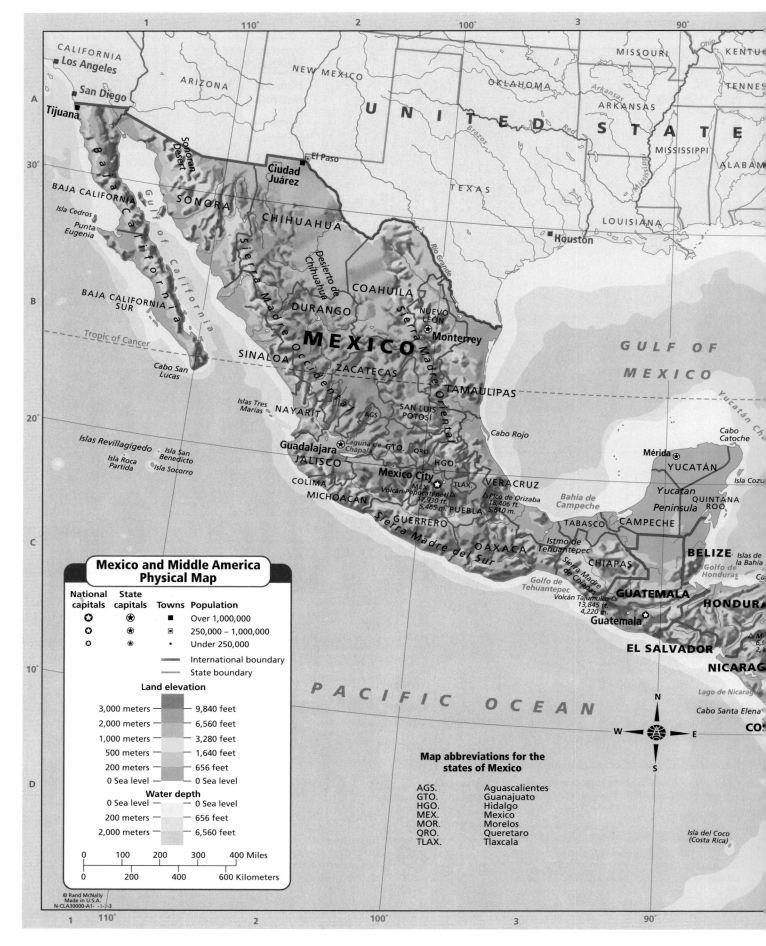

Mexico and Middle America Physical Map

National capitals	State capitals	Towns	Population
✪	✪	■	Over 1,000,000
✪	✪	▣	250,000 – 1,000,000
✪	✪	•	Under 250,000

International boundary
State boundary

Land elevation

3,000 meters	9,840 feet
2,000 meters	6,560 feet
1,000 meters	3,280 feet
500 meters	1,640 feet
200 meters	656 feet
0 Sea level	0 Sea level

Water depth

0 Sea level	0 Sea level
200 meters	656 feet
2,000 meters	6,560 feet

0   100   200   300   400 Miles
0   200   400   600 Kilometers

© Rand McNally
Made in U.S.A.
N-CLA30000-A1- -3-3-3

Map abbreviations for the states of Mexico

AGS.	Aguascalientes
GTO.	Guanajuato
HGO.	Hidalgo
MEX.	Mexico
MOR.	Morelos
QRO.	Queretaro
TLAX.	Tlaxcala

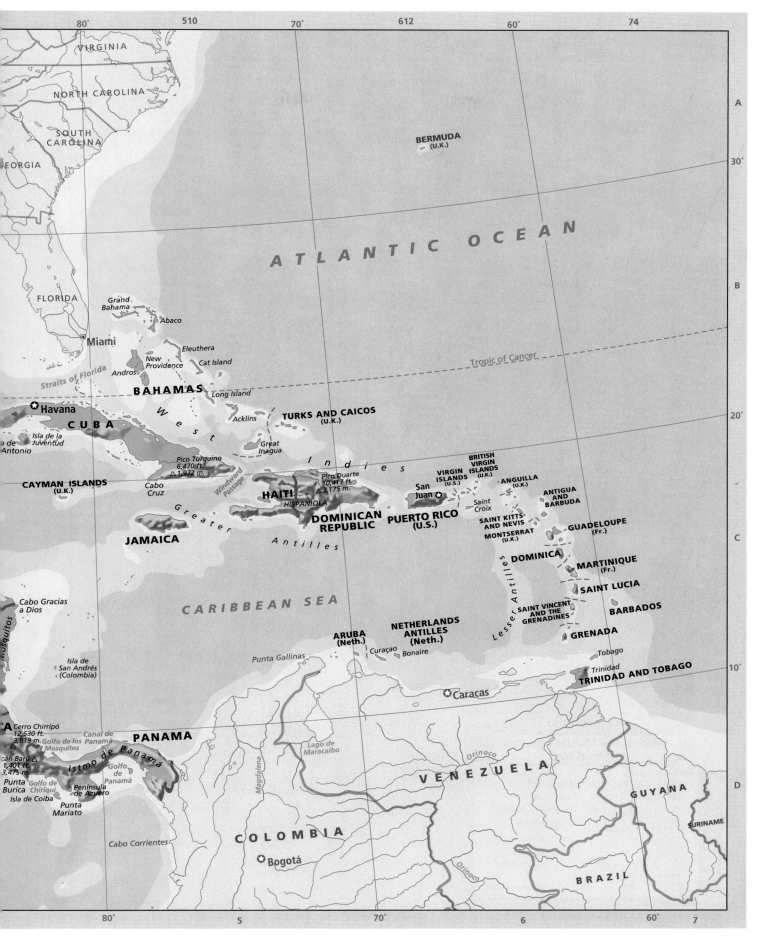

80°   510   70°   612   60°   74

VIRGINIA

NORTH CAROLINA

SOUTH CAROLINA

GEORGIA

A

30°

BERMUDA
(U.K.)

A T L A N T I C   O C E A N

B

FLORIDA

Grand
Bahama

Abaco

Miami

Eleuthera

New
Providence   Cat Island

Andros

Straits of Florida

BAHAMAS   Long Island

Tropic of Cancer

Havana

CUBA

Isla de la
Juventud

o de
Antonio

West

Acklins

Great
Inagua

TURKS AND CAICOS
(U.K.)

20°

Indies

BRITISH
VIRGIN
ISLANDS
VIRGIN   (U.K.)
ISLANDS
(U.S.)   ANGUILLA
(U.K.)

Pico Turquino
6,470 ft.
△1,972 m.

CAYMAN ISLANDS
(U.K.)

Cabo
Cruz

Windward Passage

HAITI

HISPANIOLA

Pico Duarte
10,417 ft.
△3,175 m.

San
Juan

DOMINICAN
REPUBLIC

PUERTO RICO
(U.S.)

Saint
Croix

ANTIGUA
AND
BARBUDA

SAINT KITTS
AND NEVIS

MONTSERRAT
(U.K.)

GUADELOUPE
(Fr.)

Greater

JAMAICA

Antilles

DOMINICA

MARTINIQUE
(Fr.)

SAINT LUCIA

C

Lesser Antilles

Cabo Gracias
a Dios

CARIBBEAN SEA

SAINT VINCENT
AND THE
GRENADINES

BARBADOS

Mosquitos

Isla de
San Andrés
(Colombia)

ARUBA
(Neth.)

Punta Gallinas

NETHERLANDS
ANTILLES
(Neth.)

Curaçao   Bonaire

GRENADA

Tobago

Trinidad   TRINIDAD AND TOBAGO

10°

Caracas

A Cerro Chirripó
12,530 ft.
3,819 m. Golfo de los
△ Mosquitos

Canal de
Panamá

PANAMA

Lago de
Maracaibo

Orinoco

an Barú △
1,401 ft.
3,475 m.

Istmo de Panamá

Golfo
de
Panamá

Magdalena

V E N E Z U E L A

GUYANA

Punta   Golfo de
Burica   Chiriquí
Isla de Coiba

Península
de Azuero

Punta
Mariato

COLOMBIA

Orinoco

SURINAME

D

Cabo Corrientes

Bogotá

B R A Z I L

80°   5   70°   6   60°   7

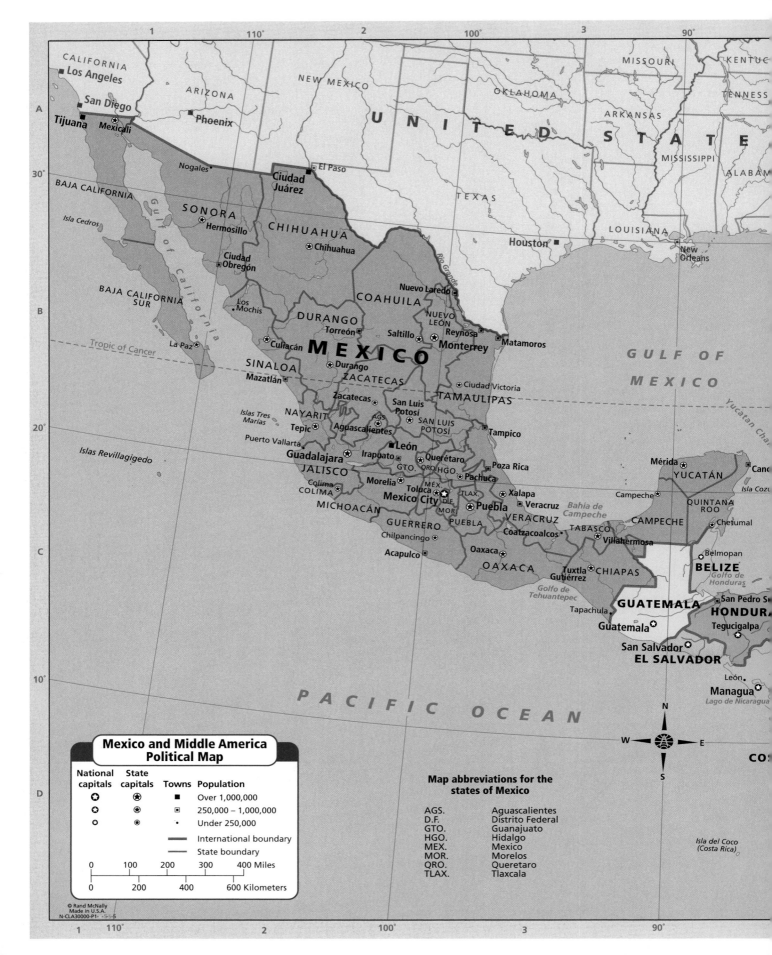

Mexico and Middle America Political Map

National capitals	State capitals	Towns	Population
☻	✪	■	Over 1,000,000
☻	✪	⊡	250,000 – 1,000,000
☻	✪	•	Under 250,000

─── International boundary
─── State boundary

| 0 | 100 | 200 | 300 | 400 Miles |

| 0 | 200 | 400 | 600 Kilometers |

© Rand McNally
Made in U.S.A.
N-CLA30000-P1- -5-5-5

Map abbreviations for the states of Mexico

AGS.	Aguascalientes
D.F.	Distrito Federal
GTO.	Guanajuato
HGO.	Hidalgo
MEX.	Mexico
MOR.	Morelos
QRO.	Queretaro
TLAX.	Tlaxcala

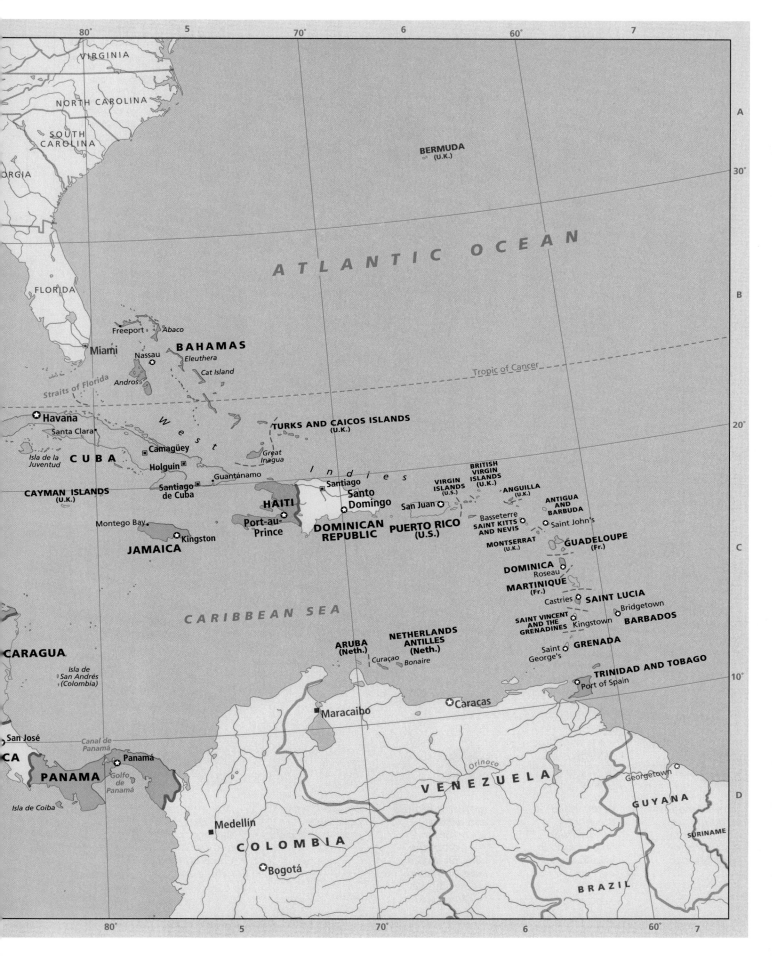

VIRGINIA

NORTH CAROLINA

SOUTH CAROLINA

ORGIA

FLORIDA

BERMUDA
(U.K.)

ATLANTIC OCEAN

A

30°

Freeport
Abaco
BAHAMAS
Miami
Nassau
Eleuthera
Cat Island
Straits of Florida
Andros

B

Tropic of Cancer

Havana
Santa Clara
West
Indies
TURKS AND CAICOS ISLANDS
(U.K.)

20°

Isla de la
Juventud
CUBA
Camagüey
Holguín
Great
Inagua
BRITISH
VIRGIN
ISLANDS
(U.K.)
ANGUILLA
(U.K.)
ANTIGUA
AND
BARBUDA

CAYMAN ISLANDS
(U.K.)
Guantánamo
Santiago
de Cuba
Santiago
Santo
Domingo
San Juan
VIRGIN
ISLANDS
(U.S.)
Basseterre
SAINT KITTS
AND NEVIS
Saint John's

HAITI
Port-au-
Prince
DOMINICAN
REPUBLIC
PUERTO RICO
(U.S.)
MONTSERRAT
(U.K.)
GUADELOUPE
(Fr.)

C

Montego Bay
Kingston
JAMAICA
DOMINICA
Roseau
MARTINIQUE
(Fr.)
Castries
SAINT LUCIA
Bridgetown

CARIBBEAN SEA
SAINT VINCENT
AND THE
GRENADINES
Kingstown
BARBADOS

CARAGUA
Isla de
San Andrés
(Colombia)
ARUBA
(Neth.)
NETHERLANDS
ANTILLES
(Neth.)
Curaçao
Bonaire
Saint
George's
GRENADA

TRINIDAD AND TOBAGO

10°

San José
Canal de
Panamá
Panamá
Port of Spain

CA
PANAMA
Golfo
de
Panamá
Maracaibo
Caracas

Isla de Coiba
Orinoco
VENEZUELA
Georgetown
GUYANA

D

Medellín
SURINAME

COLOMBIA

Bogotá
BRAZIL

80°
5
70°
6
60°
7

Population

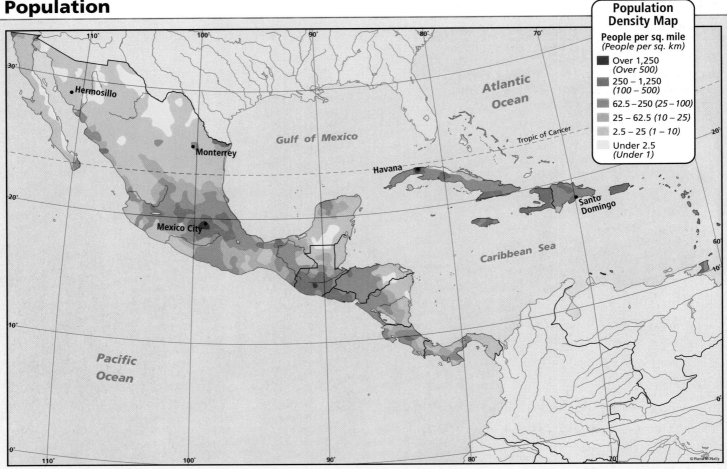

Population Density Map

People per sq. mile
(People per sq. km)

⬛	Over 1,250 *(Over 500)*
⬛	250 – 1,250 *(100 – 500)*
⬛	62.5 – 250 *(25 – 100)*
⬜	25 – 62.5 *(10 – 25)*
⬜	2.5 – 25 *(1 – 10)*
⬜	Under 2.5 *(Under 1)*

Comparing Urban and Rural Population

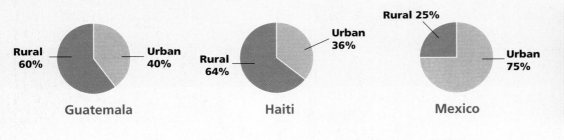

Guatemala — Rural 60%, Urban 40%

Haiti — Rural 64%, Urban 36%

Mexico — Rural 25%, Urban 75%

Mexico City is home to nearly one-fifth of Mexico's people.

A Timeline of Mexico City, Mexico

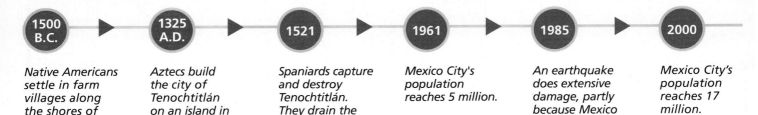

1500 B.C.
Native Americans settle in farm villages along the shores of Lake Texcoco.

1325 A.D.
Aztecs build the city of Tenochtitlán on an island in Lake Texcoco.

1521
Spaniards capture and destroy Tenochtitlán. They drain the lake, fill it with land, and build a new city they call Mexico City.

1961
Mexico City's population reaches 5 million.

1985
An earthquake does extensive damage, partly because Mexico City is built on soft, spongy soil.

2000
Mexico City's population reaches 17 million.

Economies

Per capita income is one way of measuring the relative wealth of countries. This graph compares the per capita income of six countries in Middle America. It shows how greatly wealth varies across the region, from relatively rich countries like Aruba to poor countries like Haiti.

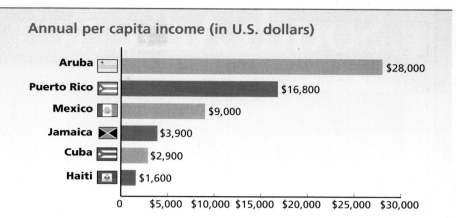

Annual per capita income (in U.S. dollars)

Aruba	$28,000
Puerto Rico	$16,800
Mexico	$9,000
Jamaica	$3,900
Cuba	$2,900
Haiti	$1,600

Environments

Cactuses grow in the hot, dry climate of Baja California, Mexico.

Tropical rain forest covers much of central America.

Palm trees flourish in the warm climate of the Caribbean Sea.

Transportation

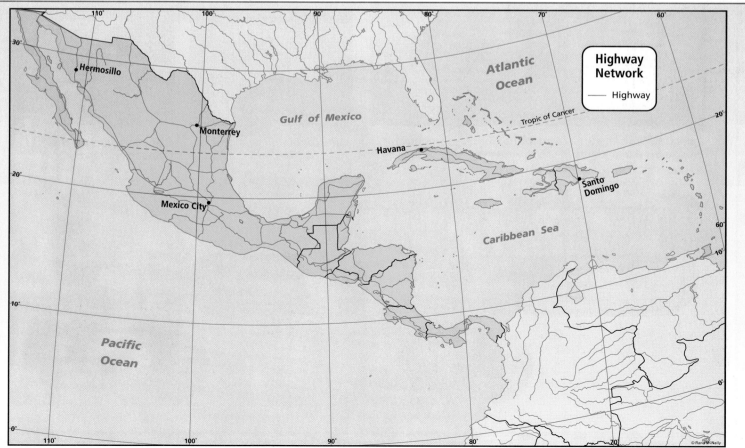

South America

South America is a continent of extremes. The Andes Mountains stretch 4,500 miles (7,200 kilometers) from north to south. They form the longest mountain chain in the world. Lake Titicaca, on the Peru-Bolivia border, is the highest lake in the world used for transportation. Arica, Chile, experienced the longest dry period ever recorded: No rain fell there for more than 14 years!

The Amazon River has the greatest volume of water of any river in the world. The Amazon discharges so much water into the Atlantic that it changes the color of the ocean's water for more than 100 miles (160 kilometers) off the shore.

Most South Americans live in cities that are major ports or are near major ports. São Paulo and Rio de Janeiro, Brazil, and Buenos Aires, Argentina, are among the world's largest cities. Altogether, almost 367 million people live in South America.

Iguacu Falls on the Brazil-Argentina border is among the most spectacular sights in South America.

Colorful buildings in Buenos Aires, Argentina

Giant tortoises on the Galapagos Islands

A Historical Look At South America

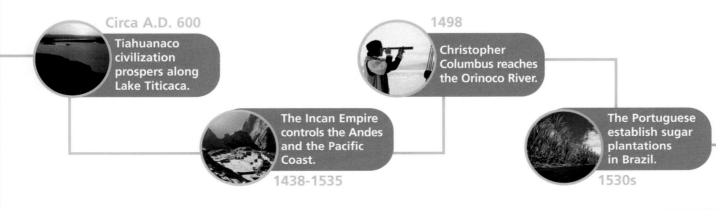

Circa A.D. 600
Tiahuanaco civilization prospers along Lake Titicaca.

1498
Christopher Columbus reaches the Orinoco River.

The Incan Empire controls the Andes and the Pacific Coast.
1438-1535

The Portuguese establish sugar plantations in Brazil.
1530s

Rain Forests

A rain forest is a dense forest that receives at least 100 inches (254 centimeters) of rain a year. The Amazon rain forest is rich in plant and animal life, and new species are discovered almost daily. Scientists have learned that many of the plants can be used to produce life-saving drugs.

However, the rain forest is disappearing. It once covered more than 2.7 million square miles (7 million square kilometers). Through a process called "deforestation," more than 12% of the rain forest has been cleared for farming, mining, and grazing.

Did You Know?

The Amazon River in South America is longer than any other river in the world except the Nile River in Africa.

Rain Forests

Deforested areas

Remaining rain forest

Sights of the Andes Mountains

More than 40 peaks in the Andes rise 20,000 feet (6,000 meters) or higher. Mining is important in the Andes, and tourism is a growing industry.

The ancient Incan city of Machu Picchu, Peru

Lake Titicaca on the Peru-Bolivia border

Fitzroy National Park in Argentina

The South American llama, a relative of the camel

1580 Spaniards found the city of Buenos Aires in Argentina.

1770s The first coffee plantations are established in Brazil.

1997 Brazil establishes the world's largest rain forest reserve.

2004 South America's population reaches 350 million.

South America Physical Map

National capitals
- ✪ Over 1,000,000
- ✪ 250,000 – 1,000,000
- ✪ Under 250,000

Towns **Population**
- ■ Over 1,000,000
- ▣ 250,000 – 1,000,000
- • Under 250,000

— International boundary

Land elevation

3,000 meters	9,840 feet
2,000 meters	6,560 feet
1,000 meters	3,280 feet
500 meters	1,640 feet
200 meters	656 feet
0 Sea level	0 Sea level

Water depth

0 Sea level	0 Sea level
200 meters	656 feet
2,000 meters	6,560 feet

0   200   400   600   800   1000 Miles
0   300   600   900   1200   1500 Kilometers

© Rand McNally
Made in U.S.A.
N-CLA40000-A1 -1-1-1

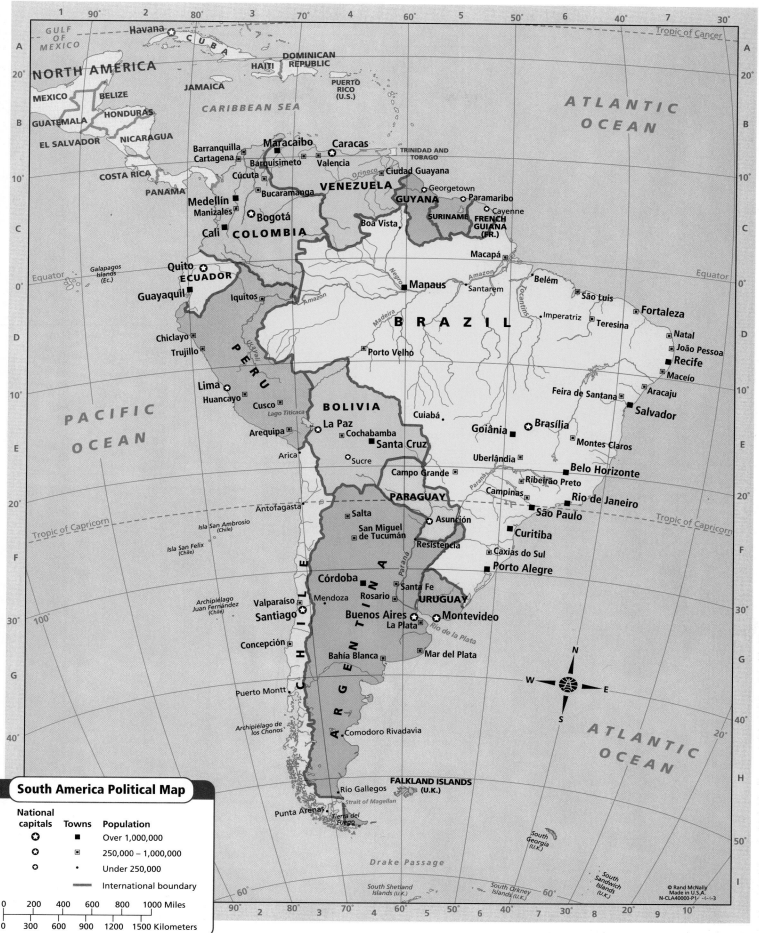

South America Political Map

National capitals
- ✪ Over 1,000,000
- ✪ 250,000 – 1,000,000
- ✪ Under 250,000

Towns   **Population**
- ■ Over 1,000,000
- ▫ 250,000 – 1,000,000
- • Under 250,000

—— International boundary

0   200   400   600   800   1000 Miles

0   300   600   900   1200   1500 Kilometers

© Rand McNally
Made in U.S.A.
N-CLA40000-P1-4-4-3

Natural Hazards

Climate

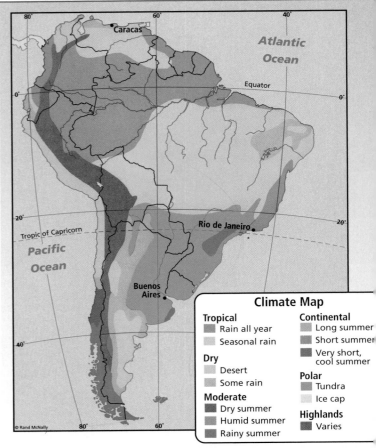

Natural Hazards Map
- Earthquakes*
- △ Volcanoes*
- \ Tsunamis
- ↖ Tropical storm tracks (over 5 per year)

*Since 1900

Climate Map

Tropical
- Rain all year
- Seasonal rain

Dry
- Desert
- Some rain

Moderate
- Dry summer
- Humid summer
- Rainy summer

Continental
- Long summer
- Short summer
- Very short, cool summer

Polar
- Tundra
- Ice cap

Highlands
- Varies

Environments

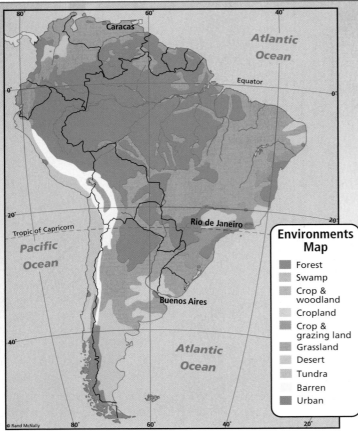

Environments Map
- Forest
- Swamp
- Crop & woodland
- Cropland
- Crop & grazing land
- Grassland
- Desert
- Tundra
- Barren
- Urban

The Amazon rain forest supports almost half of Earth's animal and plant species.

What If?

What could happen if all of the rain forests in South America are destroyed?

Population

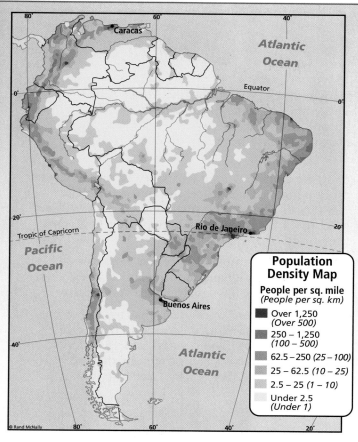

Most Brazilians live in large cities such as Rio de Janeiro.

Roughly two out of five South Americans are under the age of 20.

Did You Know?

São Paulo, Brazil, is South America's largest city.

Population Density Map

People per sq. mile
(People per sq. km)

- Over 1,250 *(Over 500)*
- 250 – 1,250 *(100 – 500)*
- 62.5 – 250 *(25 – 100)*
- 25 – 62.5 *(10 – 25)*
- 2.5 – 25 *(1 – 10)*
- Under 2.5 *(Under 1)*

Cusco, Peru, was once capital of the Incan empire.

Dense vegetation is a barrier to settlement in the Amazon River basin.

Economies

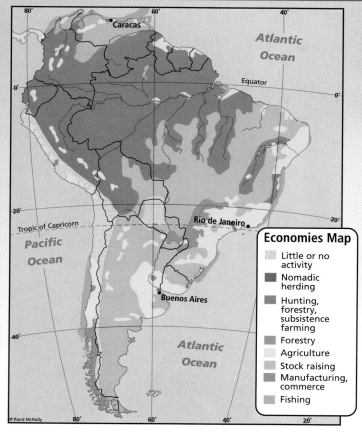

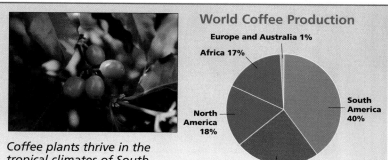

Coffee plants thrive in the tropical climates of South America.

World Coffee Production

- Europe and Australia 1%
- Africa 17%
- North America 18%
- Asia 24%
- South America 40%

Economies Map

- Little or no activity
- Nomadic herding
- Hunting, forestry, subsistence farming
- Forestry
- Agriculture
- Stock raising
- Manufacturing, commerce
- Fishing

Gross Domestic Product (GDP) in billions of U.S. dollars

Gross Domestic Product is the total value of all goods and services produced by a country in one year.

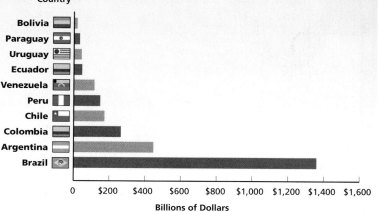

Country: Bolivia, Paraguay, Uruguay, Ecuador, Venezuela, Peru, Chile, Colombia, Argentina, Brazil

Billions of Dollars (0, $200, $400, $600, $800, $1,000, $1,200, $1,400, $1,600)

Europe

Do you know what a *lago* is? A *lac*? A *loch*? These are just some of the words for "lake" in Europe. Europe is the world's second-smallest continent, but it has many countries and many languages.

Only the giant continents of Asia and Africa have more people than Europe. Because more than 729,000,000 live in the small continent of Europe, it is one of the most densely populated regions in the world.

The two smallest countries of the world are in Europe. Vatican City and Monaco are each less than one square mile (2.6 square kilometers) in size.

In the 1990s, there were great changes in Europe. East and West Germany were reunited after 45 years. The Soviet Union divided into 15 different countries. Czechoslovakia peacefully divided into two new countries: The Czech Republic and Slovakia.

In 1991-1992, Slovenia, Croatia, Macedonia, and Bosnia and Herzegovina broke away from Yugoslavia to become independent countries. War broke out in Croatia and Bosnia. In 2003, Yugoslavia changed its name to Serbia and Montenegro.

Prague, Czech Republic

Church in the Alps, Austria

Hilltop village in Spain

Donkey and farmhouse, Aran Islands, Ireland

Did You Know?

Four European countries—Norway, Sweden, Finland, and Russia—lie partly within the Arctic Circle.

A Historical Look At Europe

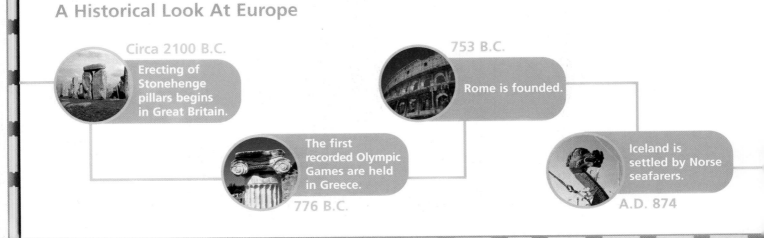

Circa 2100 B.C. Erecting of Stonehenge pillars begins in Great Britain.

776 B.C. The first recorded Olympic Games are held in Greece.

753 B.C. Rome is founded.

A.D. 874 Iceland is settled by Norse seafarers.

The European Union

Twenty-five nations have joined the European Union to form a single, powerful market for business and trade.

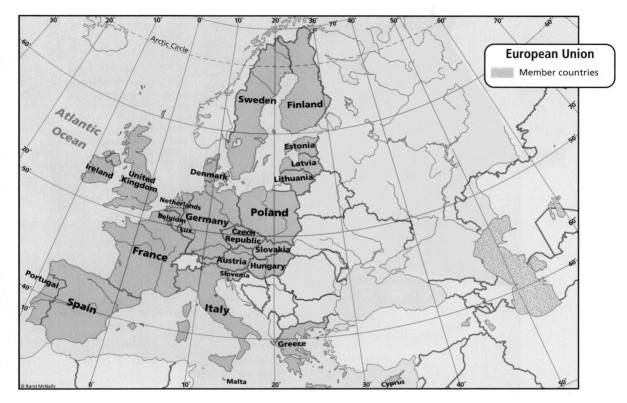

The European Union
▨ Member countries

The headquarters of the European Union is in Brussels, Belgium.

Some countries of the European Union use the euro as their currency.

Because Europe has so many languages, there are 20 official languages of the European Union.

The European Union has its own passports. Citizens of all countries can move freely around the entire area.

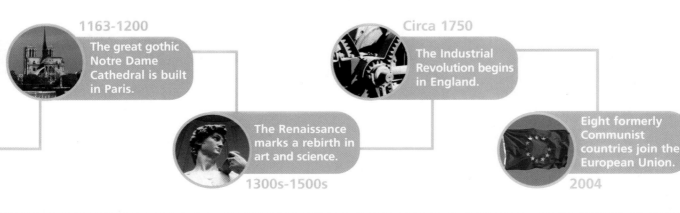

1163-1200
The great gothic Notre Dame Cathedral is built in Paris.

Circa 1750
The Industrial Revolution begins in England.

The Renaissance marks a rebirth in art and science.
1300s-1500s

Eight formerly Communist countries join the European Union.
2004

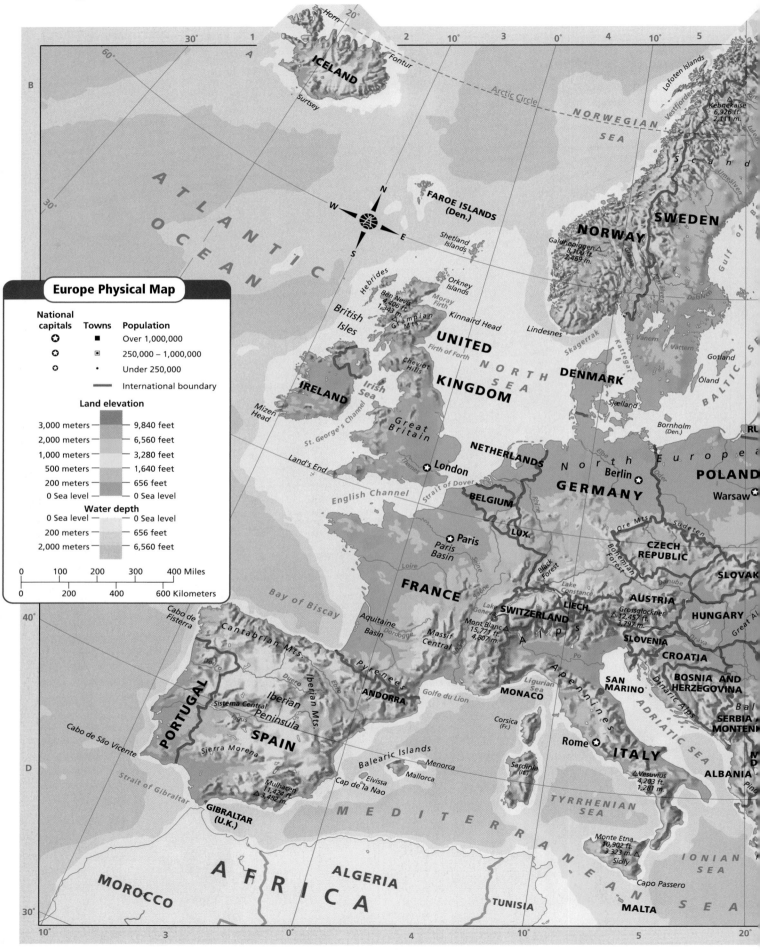

Europe Physical Map

National capitals
- ✪ Over 1,000,000
- ✪ 250,000 – 1,000,000
- ✪ Under 250,000

Towns Population
- ■ Over 1,000,000
- ▣ 250,000 – 1,000,000
- • Under 250,000
- ── International boundary

Land elevation

3,000 meters	9,840 feet
2,000 meters	6,560 feet
1,000 meters	3,280 feet
500 meters	1,640 feet
200 meters	656 feet
0 Sea level	0 Sea level

Water depth

0 Sea level	0 Sea level
200 meters	656 feet
2,000 meters	6,560 feet

0 100 200 300 400 Miles
0 200 400 600 Kilometers

Murmansk

Kola
Peninsula

WHITE SEA

Ponoy

Mezen

Timan Ridge

Pechora

Gora Narodnaya
6,214 ft.
1,894 m.

Ural Mountains

Ob'

Irtysh

60°

80°

B

FINLAND

Severnaya Dvina

Sukhona

Lake
Onega

Finland

Lake
Ladoga

Severnyye Uvaly
(Hills)

*Kama
Resevoir*

Kama

A S I A

50°

NIA

Lake
Peipus

*Rybinsk
Res.*

Gorki
Res.

Volga

R U S S I A

Kuybyshev
Res.

70°

ATVIA

Valdai
Hills

Moscow

Oka

Volga

C

ain

Neman

Central
Russian
Upland

Oka-Don Plain

Don

Khoper

Volga Upland

Volgograd
Res.

Ural

KAZAKHSTAN

Caspian Depression

Aral Sea

BELARUS

Prypjac

Dnieper Lowland

Donets Basin

*Tsymlyansk
Res.*

Volga

UZBEKISTAN

Amu Darya

Kiev

Dnieper

UKRAINE

40°

ster

MOLDOVA

Sea of Azov

TURKMENISTAN

60°

NIA

Crimean
Peninsula

C a u c a s u s

Gora El'brus
18,510 ft.
5,642 m.

GEORGIA

C
A
S
P
I
A
N

S
E
A

an Alps

danube

B L A C K   S E A

ARMENIA

AZERBAIJAN

AZER.

D

ninsula

BULGARIA

hodope Mts

İstanbul

IRAN

mpus
t.
tn.

Sea of
Marmara

TURKEY

ECE

AEGEAN SEA

IRAQ

Tigris

30°

Sea of Crete

Rhodes

CYPRUS

SYRIA

LEBANON

Euphrates

Crete

Europe Political Map

National capitals	State capitals	Towns	Population
✪	✪	■	Over 1,000,000
✪	✪	▣	250,000 – 1,000,000
✪	✪	•	Under 250,000

International boundary
State boundary

| 0 | 100 | 200 | 300 | 400 Miles |
| 0 | 200 | 400 | 600 Kilometers |

ICELAND
Reykjavík

FAROE ISLANDS (Den.)

Arctic Circle

NORWEGIAN SEA

Trondheim

Umeå

SWEDEN

NORWAY

Bergen

Oslo

Göteborg

Stockholm

Vänern

Vättern

Skagerrak

Kattegat

DENMARK

Copenhagen

BALTIC SEA

Kaliningrad

Gdańsk

LITHU

POLAND

Warsaw

Łódź

Szczecin

Hamburg

Berlin

GERMANY

Wrocław

Dresden

Katowice

Kra

CZECH REPUBLIC

Prague

SLOVAK

Vienna

Bratislava

AUSTRIA

Graz

Budapest

HUNGARY

Belg

SLOVENIA

Ljubljana

Zagreb

CROATIA

Venice

BOSNIA AND HERZEGOVINA

SAN MARINO

Split

Sarajevo

SERBIA MONTEN

ATLANTIC OCEAN

SCOTLAND

Aberdeen

Glasgow

Edinburgh

UNITED

NORTHERN IRELAND

Belfast

Dublin

IRELAND

Cork

Liverpool

Manchester

NORTH SEA

KINGDOM

WALES

Birmingham

ENGLAND

Cardiff

Plymouth

St. George's Channel

Irish Sea

London

Thames

Strait of Dover

NETHERLANDS

Amsterdam

The Hague

Antwerp

Essen

Cologne

Bonn

BELGIUM

Brussels

LUX.

Luxembourg

Frankfurt

English Channel

Le Havre

Brest

Paris

Nantes

Loire

Seine

Strasbourg

Rhine

Stuttgart

Munich

Zurich

Bern

LIECH.

SWITZERLAND

Geneva

Lyon

Rhône

FRANCE

Bay of Biscay

Bordeaux

Toulouse

A Coruña

Gijón

Bilbao

Valladolid

Zaragoza

ANDORRA

Porto

Ebro

PORTUGAL

Lisbon

Tagus

Madrid

SPAIN

Córdoba

València

Valencia

Seville

Alacant

Palma

Málaga

GIBRALTAR (U.K.)

Strait of Gibraltar

Algiers

Marseille

Golfe du Lion

MONACO

Nice

Turin

Milan

Genoa

Bologna

Po

Ligurian Sea

Corsica

Florence

San Marino

ITALY

Rome

VATICAN CITY

Naples

Bari

Tiranë

ALBANIA

Sardinia

Cagliari

TYRRHENIAN SEA

ADRIATIC SEA

Skop

GRE

Palermo

Messina

Sicily

Catania

IONIAN SEA

MEDITERRANEAN

SEA

MOROCCO

ALGERIA

AFRICA

TUNISIA

MALTA

7   40°   8   50°   9   60°   10   70°   11   80°

• Murmansk

WHITE SEA

• Arkhangel'sk

Pechora

• Ukhta

R U S S I A

Severnaya Dvina

Syktyvkar

• Berezniki

• Petrozavodsk
Lake
Onega

Perm'

B

FINLAND

Lake
Ladoga

• Kirov

A S I A

50°

Helsinki

• Saint Petersburg

Cherepovets
Rybinsk
Res.

Izhevsk

Naberezhnye
Chelny   Ufa

Minn

Lake
Peipus

Gorki
Res.

Nizhniy
Novgorod   Kazan'

70°

NIA

Yaroslavl'

Ivanovo

Kuybyshev
Res.

LATVIA

Tver'

Oka

Samara

Moscow

Ryazan'

Volga

Vicebsk

Penza

Tula

C

Minsk

Bryansk

Saratov

Ural

Volgograd
Res.

BELARUS

Homel'

Lipetsk

Don

K A Z A K H S T A N

Aral Sea

Chornobyl'

Voronezh

U Z B E K I S T A N

Kiev   Kharkiv

Volgograd

Atyraū

iv

Vinnytsia   UKRAINE

Dnipro-
petrovs'k

Luhans'k

Dnieper

Tsymlyansk
Res.

Volga

40°

Dniester

Kryvyi Rih

Donets'k

Astrakhan

60°

MOLDOVA

Zaporizhzhia

Mariupol'

Rostov-na-Donu

C
A
S
P
I
A
N

T U R K M E N I S T A N

Iași

Chișinău

Stavropol'

Napoca

Odesa

Krasnodar

Sea of Azov

S
E
A

MANIA

Simferopol'

Vladikavkaz

Galați

Sevastopol'

Bucharest

BLACK   SEA

GEORGIA

Tbilisi

Baku

niova

Constanța

D

BULGARIA   Varna

ARMENIA   AZERBAIJAN

fia

Yerevan   AZER.

Tehran

Plovdiv

İstanbul

Sea of
Marmara

salonîki

Ankara

TURKEY

IRAN

AEGEAN
SEA

ens

SYRIA

IRAQ

30°

Crete

CYPRUS   Baghdad

LEBANON

6   30°   7   40°   8   50°   9

Climate

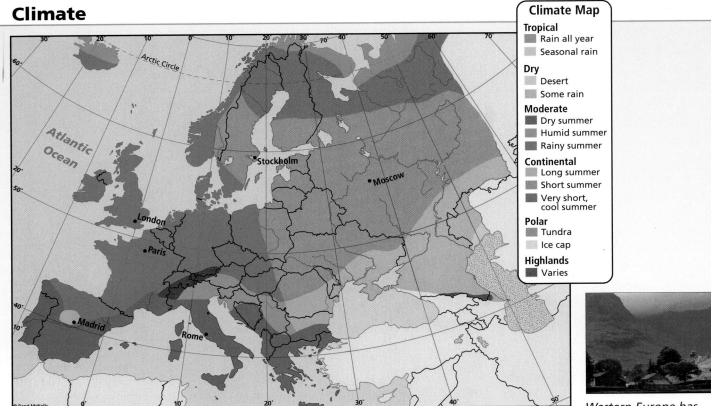

Climate Map

Tropical
- Rain all year
- Seasonal rain

Dry
- Desert
- Some rain

Moderate
- Dry summer
- Humid summer
- Rainy summer

Continental
- Long summer
- Short summer
- Very short, cool summer

Polar
- Tundra
- Ice cap

Highlands
- Varies

Western Europe has a mild, rainy climate.

Population

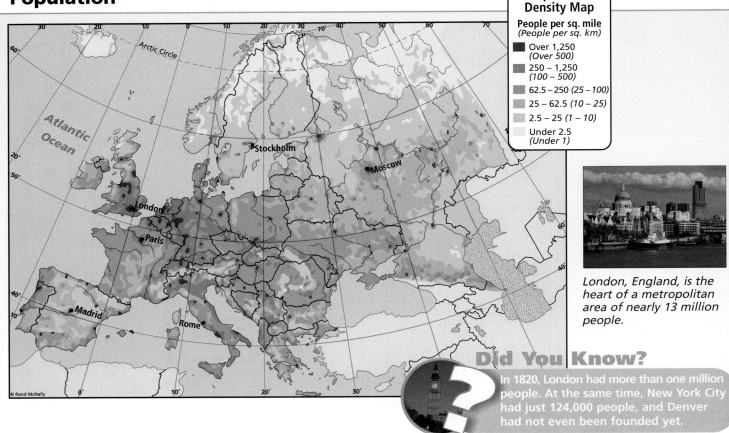

Population Density Map

People per sq. mile
(People per sq. km)

- Over 1,250 *(Over 500)*
- 250 – 1,250 *(100 – 500)*
- 62.5 – 250 *(25 – 100)*
- 25 – 62.5 *(10 – 25)*
- 2.5 – 25 *(1 – 10)*
- Under 2.5 *(Under 1)*

London, England, is the heart of a metropolitan area of nearly 13 million people.

Did You Know?

In 1820, London had more than one million people. At the same time, New York City had just 124,000 people, and Denver had not even been founded yet.

Environments

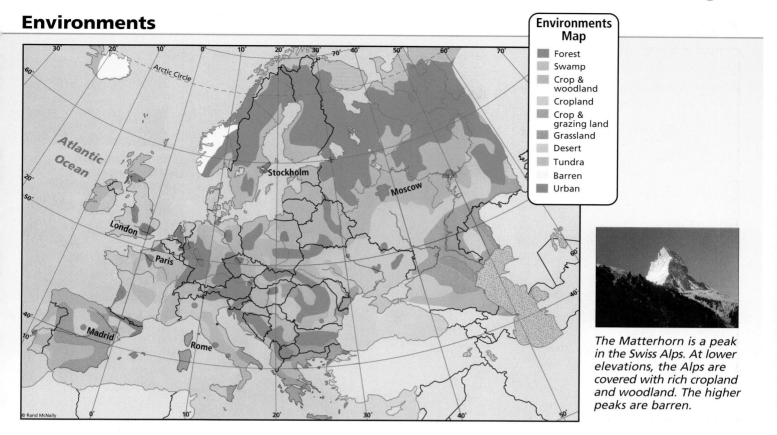

Environments Map
- Forest
- Swamp
- Crop & woodland
- Cropland
- Crop & grazing land
- Grassland
- Desert
- Tundra
- Barren
- Urban

The Matterhorn is a peak in the Swiss Alps. At lower elevations, the Alps are covered with rich cropland and woodland. The higher peaks are barren.

Economies

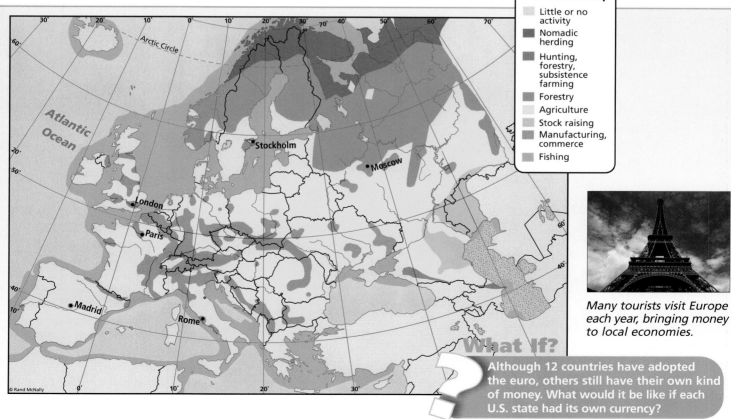

Economies Map
- Little or no activity
- Nomadic herding
- Hunting, forestry, subsistence farming
- Forestry
- Agriculture
- Stock raising
- Manufacturing, commerce
- Fishing

Many tourists visit Europe each year, bringing money to local economies.

What If?

Although 12 countries have adopted the euro, others still have their own kind of money. What would it be like if each U.S. state had its own currency?

Natural Hazards

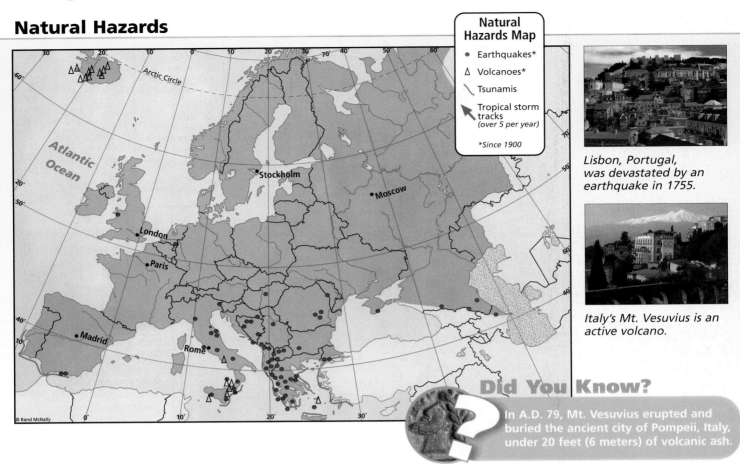

Natural Hazards Map
- Earthquakes*
- △ Volcanoes*
- Tsunamis
- ↖ Tropical storm tracks *(over 5 per year)*

*Since 1900

Lisbon, Portugal, was devastated by an earthquake in 1755.

Italy's Mt. Vesuvius is an active volcano.

Did You Know?

In A.D. 79, Mt. Vesuvius erupted and buried the ancient city of Pompeii, Italy, under 20 feet (6 meters) of volcanic ash.

Transportation

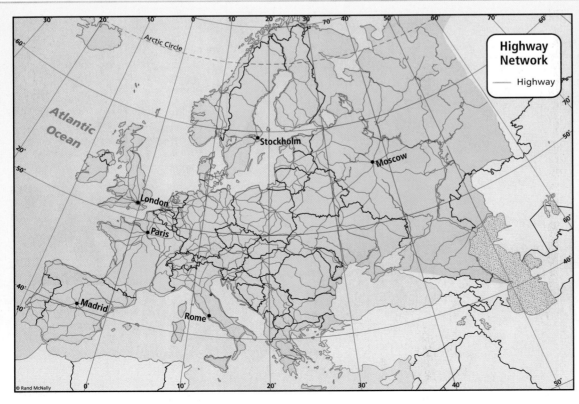

Highway Network
— Highway

A canal boat is a modern means of transportation in Amsterdam, the Netherlands.

High-speed rail systems connect many European cities.

Energy

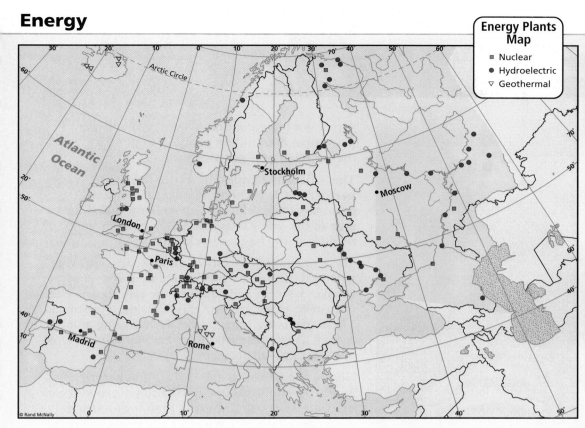

Energy Plants Map

- ■ Nuclear
- ● Hydroelectric
- ▽ Geothermal

In Iceland, water from hot springs heats homes and fuels geothermal plants.

Hydroelectric power is still important in some parts of Europe. This dam is in Switzerland.

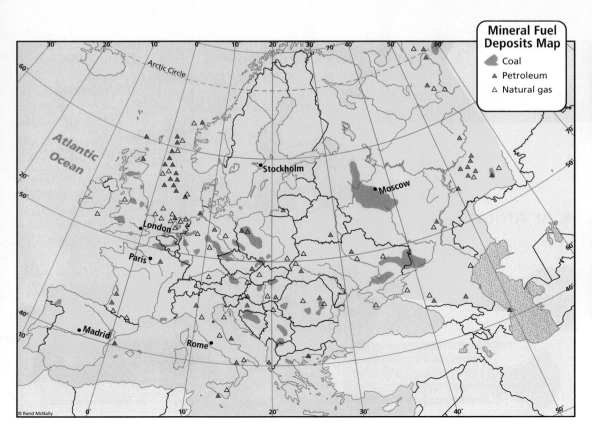

Mineral Fuel Deposits Map

- Coal
- ▲ Petroleum
- △ Natural gas

North Sea oil and gas are important sources of energy for the United Kingdom and Norway.

Coal was the first fuel for modern factories, but today it is less favored because it is so polluting.

Africa

African elephant

Africa is a huge continent. Only Asia is larger. More than 866 million people live in Africa, and the population is growing fast.

The Sahara, the largest desert in the world, covers northern Africa with sand, rock, and volcanic mountains. South of the Sahara is the Sahel, an area of dry grasslands. The Sahel expands and recedes with changes in climate.

The tropical rain forests of central Africa provide a natural habitat for gorillas, chimpanzees, and monkeys. North and south of the rain forests and in eastern Africa are vast grassy plains, or savannas. These plains are home to herds of grazing animals, as well as elephants, lions, and other animals most of us see only in zoos.

During the late 19th and early 20th centuries, European countries occupied and governed most of Africa. Today, almost every country in Africa is independent. Africa has 53 countries, the most of any continent.

Many of Africa's people are poor, and they face great challenges in health care, literacy, and life expectancy. Terrible civil wars have torn apart several nations.

Nevertheless, Africa has many possibilities. Hydroelectric power from the Congo and other rivers, minerals such as iron and copper, and improved farming methods could offer the hope of better lives to many Africans.

Did You Know?

Tectonic forces are slowly tearing Africa into two parts. The Rift Valley in eastern Africa marks the dividing line.

A Historical Look At Africa

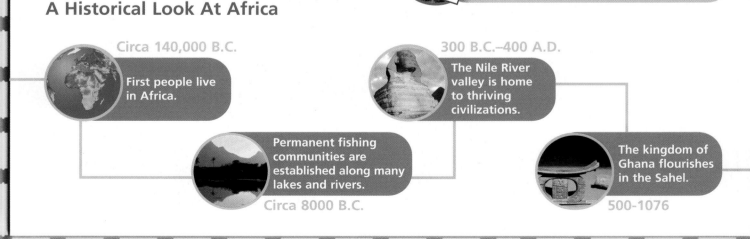

Circa 140,000 B.C.
First people live in Africa.

Circa 8000 B.C.
Permanent fishing communities are established along many lakes and rivers.

300 B.C.–400 A.D.
The Nile River valley is home to thriving civilizations.

500-1076
The kingdom of Ghana flourishes in the Sahel.

African Independence

In the late 19th and early 20th centuries, European countries had colonies in almost all of Africa. As recently as 1950, only four African countries were independent: Egypt, Ethiopia, Liberia, and South Africa. During the following decades, anti-colonial movements gathered strength across the continent. By the end of the 1970s, a total of 43 countries had become independent. Today, the only African country that is not independent is Western Sahara, which is under the control of Morocco.

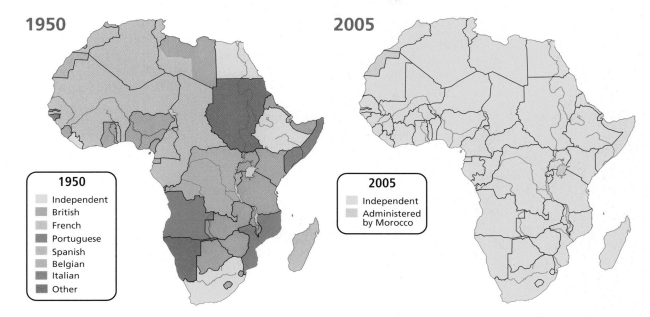

1950

1950
- Independent
- British
- French
- Portuguese
- Spanish
- Belgian
- Italian
- Other

2005

2005
- Independent
- Administered by Morocco

The People of Africa

There are more than 800 ethnic groups in Africa. It is estimated that the people of Africa speak between 800 and 1,600 different languages.

Children from Egypt

Girl from Ethiopia

Women from Mauritius

Shepherd from the Sahel

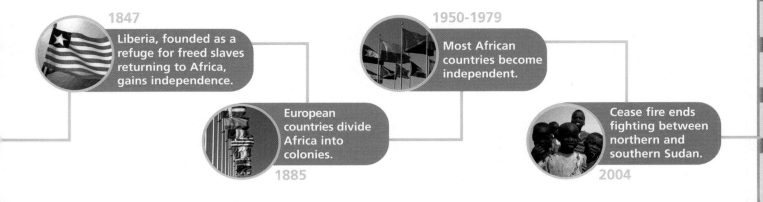

1847 Liberia, founded as a refuge for freed slaves returning to Africa, gains independence.

1885 European countries divide Africa into colonies.

1950-1979 Most African countries become independent.

2004 Cease fire ends fighting between northern and southern Sudan.

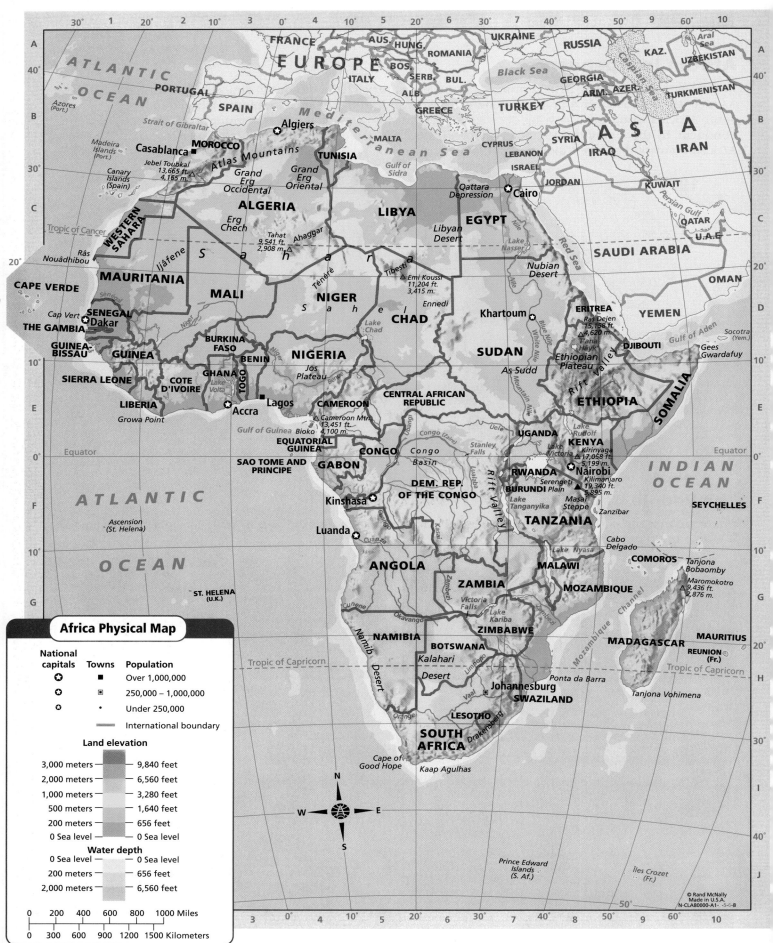

Africa Physical Map

National capitals
- ✪ Over 1,000,000
- ✪ 250,000 – 1,000,000
- ✪ Under 250,000

Towns
- ■ Over 1,000,000
- ▣ 250,000 – 1,000,000
- ▪ Under 250,000

Population

—— International boundary

Land elevation

3,000 meters	9,840 feet
2,000 meters	6,560 feet
1,000 meters	3,280 feet
500 meters	1,640 feet
200 meters	656 feet
0 Sea level	0 Sea level

Water depth

0 Sea level	0 Sea level
200 meters	656 feet
2,000 meters	6,560 feet

0 200 400 600 800 1000 Miles
0 300 600 900 1200 1500 Kilometers

© Rand McNally
Made in U.S.A.
N-CLA80000-A1- -5-6-8

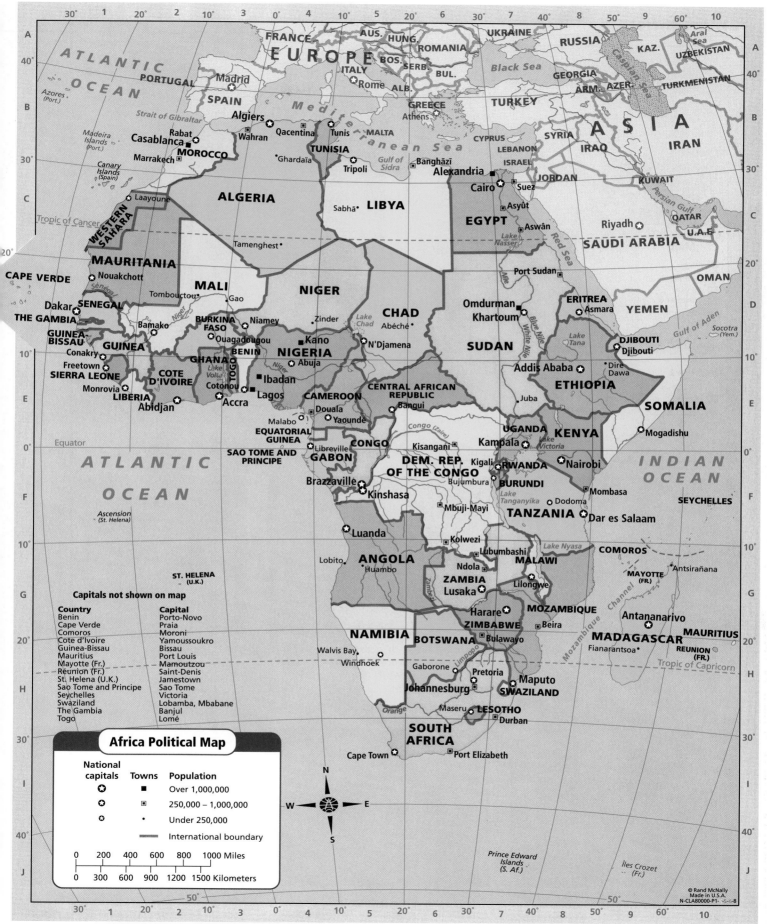

Africa Political Map

ATLANTIC OCEAN

EUROPE

FRANCE · AUS. · HUNG. · UKRAINE · RUSSIA · KAZ. · UZBEKISTAN
Madrid · ITALY · Rome · BOS. · SERB. · BUL. · ROMANIA · Black Sea · GEORGIA · ARM. · AZER. · TURKMENISTAN
PORTUGAL · SPAIN · ALB. · GREECE · Athens · TURKEY · ASIA · IRAN
Strait of Gibraltar · Mediterranean Sea · CYPRUS · SYRIA · IRAQ
Algiers · Qacentina · Tunis · MALTA · LEBANON · ISRAEL · JORDAN · KUWAIT
Rabat · Wahran · TUNISIA · Gulf of Sidra · Banghāzī · Alexandria · Cairo · Suez · Asyūt · Riyadh · QATAR · U.A.E.
Casablanca · MOROCCO · Tripoli · Aswān · SAUDI ARABIA · OMAN
Marrakech · Ghardaïa
Canary Islands (Spain) · Laayoune · ALGERIA · LIBYA · Sabhā · EGYPT · Lake Nasser · Red Sea
Tropic of Cancer · WESTERN SAHARA · Tamenghest · Port Sudan · YEMEN · Socotra (Yem.)
CAPE VERDE · MAURITANIA · Omdurman · ERITREA · Asmara · Gulf of Aden
Nouakchott · MALI · NIGER · CHAD · Khartoum · DJIBOUTI · Djibouti
Dakar · SENEGAL · Tombouctou · Gao · Zinder · Abéché · Lake Chad · N'Djamena · SUDAN · Lake Tana · Addis Ababa · Diré Dawa
THE GAMBIA · Bamako · BURKINA FASO · Niamey · Kano · Juba · ETHIOPIA
GUINEA-BISSAU · GUINEA · Ouagadougou · NIGERIA · Abuja · CENTRAL AFRICAN REPUBLIC · SOMALIA · Mogadishu
Conakry · GHANA · BENIN · Ibadan · Bangui · UGANDA · KENYA
Freetown · SIERRA LEONE · COTE D'IVOIRE · TOGO · Lagos · Douala · Yaoundé · Malabo · CAMEROON · Kampala · Lake Victoria · Nairobi
Monrovia · LIBERIA · Accra · Cotonou · EQUATORIAL GUINEA · Congo (Zaïre) · Kisangani · RWANDA · Kigali · BURUNDI
Abidjan · SAO TOME AND PRINCIPE · GABON · CONGO · Libreville · DEM. REP. OF THE CONGO · Bujumbura · Lake Tanganyika · Dodoma · Mombasa
Equator · Brazzaville · Kinshasa · Mbuji-Mayi · TANZANIA · Dar es Salaam · SEYCHELLES
Ascension (St. Helena) · Luanda · Kolwezi · Lake Nyasa · COMOROS · MAYOTTE (FR.) · Antsirañana
Lobito · ANGOLA · Huambo · Lubumbashi · Ndola · MALAWI · Lilongwe
ST. HELENA (U.K.) · ZAMBIA · Lusaka · MOZAMBIQUE · Antananarivo
NAMIBIA · Harare · ZIMBABWE · Beira · MADAGASCAR · MAURITIUS · REUNION (FR.)
Walvis Bay · BOTSWANA · Bulawayo · Fianarantsoa · Tropic of Capricorn
Windhoek · Gaborone · Limpopo · Mozambique Channel
Johannesburg · Pretoria · Maputo · SWAZILAND
Maseru · LESOTHO · Durban
SOUTH AFRICA
Cape Town · Port Elizabeth

INDIAN OCEAN

Capitals not shown on map

Country	Capital
Benin	Porto-Novo
Cape Verde	Praia
Comoros	Moroni
Cote d'Ivoire	Yamoussoukro
Guinea-Bissau	Bissau
Mauritius	Port Louis
Mayotte (Fr.)	Mamoutzou
Réunion (Fr.)	Saint-Denis
St. Helena (U.K.)	Jamestown
Sao Tome and Principe	Sao Tome
Seychelles	Victoria
Swaziland	Lobamba, Mbabane
The Gambia	Banjul
Togo	Lomé

Africa Political Map

National capitals · Towns · Population
⊕ · ■ · Over 1,000,000
⊕ · ⊡ · 250,000 – 1,000,000
⊕ · · · Under 250,000
━━━ · International boundary

N W E S

0 200 400 600 800 1000 Miles
0 300 600 900 1200 1500 Kilometers

Prince Edward Islands (S. Af.) · Îles Crozet (Fr.)

© Rand McNally
Made in U.S.A.
N-CLA80000-P1- -5-6-8

Environments

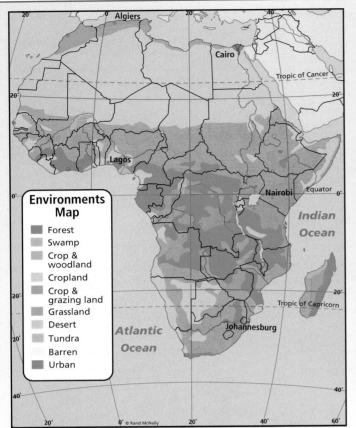

Tropical rain forests of central Africa are hot and humid. Jungles are areas of dense, tangled plant growth in these forests.

An erg is a large area of sand dunes in a desert. Deserts cover about one-third of Africa.

Savannas, areas of grassland with few trees, cover about 40% of Africa's land area. Similar areas in North America are called prairies.

The Sahel borders the Sahara on the south. Rainfall varies greatly from year to year, and growing population has led to overfarming and overgrazing. The Sahel suffers from desertification.

An oasis in a desert is found where underground water comes to the surface.

Although many Africans still live in the countryside, Africa has large, modern cities. This is a view of Johannesburg, South Africa.

Africa's most fertile cropland is found along its rivers. This farm is in Egypt's Nile River valley.

Climate

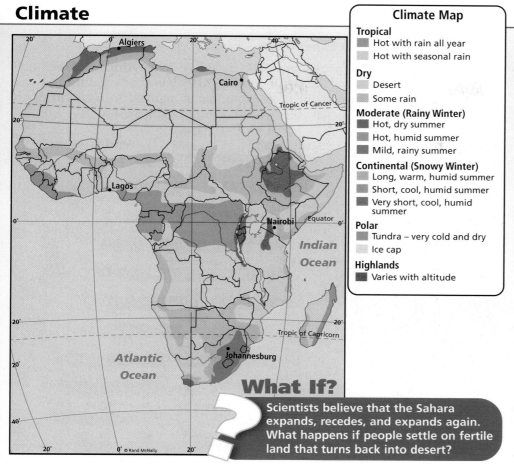

Climate Map

Tropical
- Hot with rain all year
- Hot with seasonal rain

Dry
- Desert
- Some rain

Moderate (Rainy Winter)
- Hot, dry summer
- Hot, humid summer
- Mild, rainy summer

Continental (Snowy Winter)
- Long, warm, humid summer
- Short, cool, humid summer
- Very short, cool, humid summer

Polar
- Tundra – very cold and dry
- Ice cap

Highlands
- Varies with altitude

The Sahara

The Sahara is the largest hot desert in the world. It covers about two-and-a-half million square miles (six million square kilometers). The name "Sahara" comes from the Arabic word for desert.

The highest temperature ever recorded in the world was in the Sahara: 136° F (58° C). But the Sahara can be very cold at night because the dry air does not hold much heat. The daytime and nighttime temperatures can differ by as much as 100° F (56° C).

On average, rainfall in the Sahara is less than 10 inches (25 centimeters) per year. There may be no rain at all for years at a time.

Besides sand, the Sahara has vast areas of gravel, rocky plateaus, and volcanic mountains.

What If?

? Scientists believe that the Sahara expands, recedes, and expands again. What happens if people settle on fertile land that turns back into desert?

Animals of the Savanna

African elephants

Lion

Thomson's gazelles

White rhinoceroses

Cheetah and cubs

Zebras

Natural Hazards

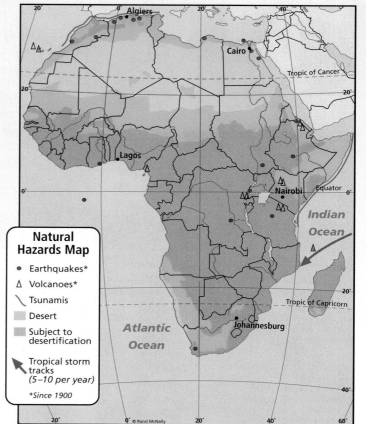

Natural Hazards Map

- • Earthquakes*
- △ Volcanoes*
- ╲ Tsunamis
- Desert
- Subject to desertification
- ➴ Tropical storm tracks (5–10 per year)

*Since 1900

Population

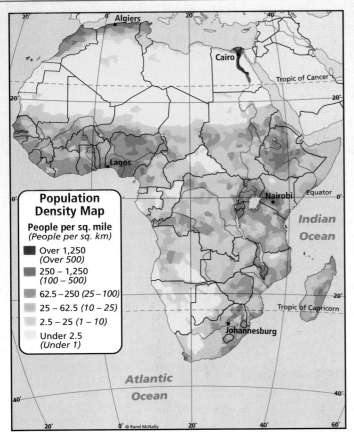

Population Density Map

People per sq. mile
(People per sq. km)

- Over 1,250 *(Over 500)*
- 250 – 1,250 *(100 – 500)*
- 62.5 – 250 *(25 – 100)*
- 25 – 62.5 *(10 – 25)*
- 2.5 – 25 *(1 – 10)*
- Under 2.5 *(Under 1)*

Life Expectancy

Life expectancy varies widely across Africa. In recent years, the deadly disease AIDS has shortened the average life span of people in many African countries, especially those south of the Sahara Desert.

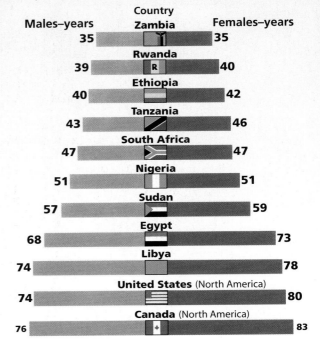

Males–years	Country	Females–years
35	Zambia	35
39	Rwanda	40
40	Ethiopia	42
43	Tanzania	46
47	South Africa	47
51	Nigeria	51
57	Sudan	59
68	Egypt	73
74	Libya	78
74	United States (North America)	80
76	Canada (North America)	83

Transportation

Did You Know?

During the 1967 war with Israel, Egypt sank ships in the Suez Canal to block traffic. The canal stayed closed for eight years.

Fewer than 10% of the roads in Africa are paved.

Camels are still used to transport goods across the desert. Their heavy-lidded eyes and closeable nostrils offer protection in sandstorms, and they can travel long distances without water.

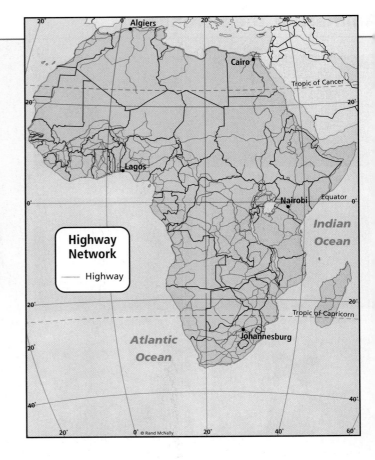

Highway Network

— Highway

Economies

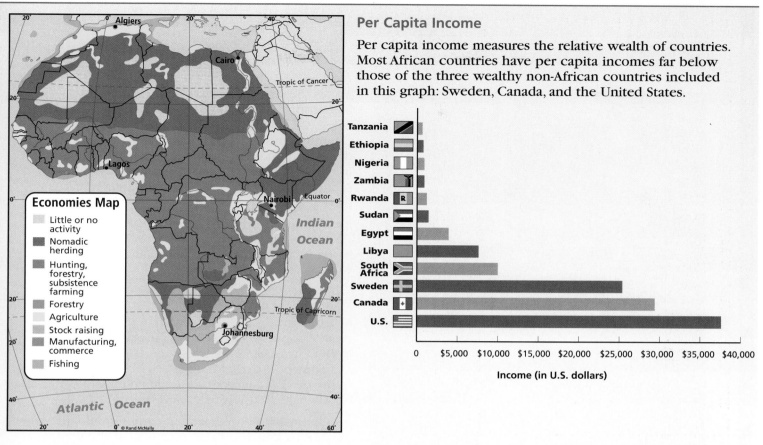

Per Capita Income

Per capita income measures the relative wealth of countries. Most African countries have per capita incomes far below those of the three wealthy non-African countries included in this graph: Sweden, Canada, and the United States.

Economies Map
- Little or no activity
- Nomadic herding
- Hunting, forestry, subsistence farming
- Forestry
- Agriculture
- Stock raising
- Manufacturing, commerce
- Fishing

Income (in U.S. dollars)

In many parts of Africa, nomadic herding is the way of life for most people.

The monuments of ancient Egypt attract millions of visitors each year. Tourism revenue is an important contributor to Egypt's economy.

About three-quarters of all Africans make a living by farming.

World Gold Production
- South Africa 17%
- All other countries 40%
- United States 13%
- Australia 11%
- China 7%
- Canada 6%
- Russia 6%

World Platinum Production
- All other countries 10%
- Russia 34%
- South Africa 56%

World Diamond Production
- All other countries 4%
- Russia 20%
- Africa 53%
- Australia / Oceania 23%

One reason for the high annual per capita income for South Africa is that it is rich in gold, platinum, and diamonds. Discovery of these precious mineral resources in the 1800s brought many Europeans to settle in South Africa.

Asia

Asia is the world's largest continent, and it is immense. It covers more than 17 million square miles (44 million square kilometers). It stretches from the sands of the Middle Eastern deserts in the west to the island country of Japan in the east. In the north, Siberian Russia extends beyond the Arctic Circle, while in the south Indonesia reaches the equator.

Asia is home to some of the world's oldest civilizations. Farming, cities, and writing began in Mesopotamia, in the Indus River valley, and in China thousands of years ago. Asians also invented many things that we use today, such as the idea of zero, paper, the printing press, and the magnetic compass.

Many countries in Asia are working to develop their economies, and their people still have difficult lives. Other Asian countries such as Japan, Taiwan, and Singapore are economic powers. The fortunes of the oil-rich countries of the Middle East depend on the value of their oil exports.

Asia has more people than any other continent: 3.8 billion, which is more than 60% of the world's people. China alone has 1.3 billion people, and India has passed one billion. Eastern China is as densely populated as the New York City urban area.

Terraced rice field in Bali, Indonesia

Mt. Fuji in Japan

Limestone pinnacles along the Li River in China

Did You Know?

The highest point in the world (Mt. Everest) and the lowest point (the Dead Sea) are both in Asia.

A Historical Look At Asia

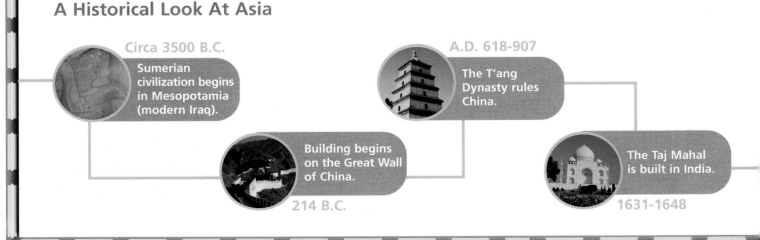

Circa 3500 B.C.
Sumerian civilization begins in Mesopotamia (modern Iraq).

214 B.C.
Building begins on the Great Wall of China.

A.D. 618-907
The T'ang Dynasty rules China.

1631-1648
The Taj Mahal is built in India.

The Regions of Asia

Asia is divided into several regions. Use the political map on pages 94 and 95 to determine the countries in each region.

Central Asia
Central Asia is rugged and dry. Farming in most places is difficult, and many people make a living as nomadic herders. The region may have large deposits of oil.

Southwest Asia
Most of Southwest Asia is desert and semi-desert. The region has the world's richest deposits of oil.

South Asia
India and neighboring countries make up South Asia. The Himalayas border the northeastern part of this region.

North Asia
North Asia has long, bitterly cold winters. Despite its mineral resources, fewer people live in North Asia than in any other part of the continent.

East Asia
Eastern China and its neighbors make up East Asia. About one quarter of the world's people live in East Asia.

Southeast Asia
A part of the Asian mainland and many islands make up Southeast Asia. Most of the region has a tropical climate.

Central Asia

Southwest Asia

South Asia

North Asia

East Asia

Southeast Asia

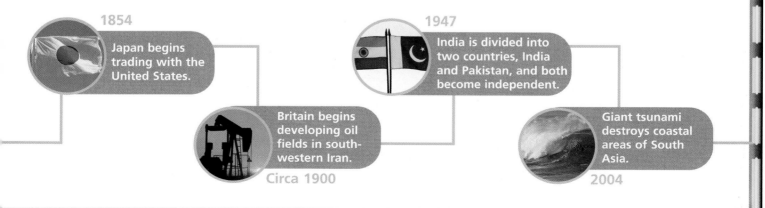

1854 Japan begins trading with the United States.

Circa 1900 Britain begins developing oil fields in south-western Iran.

1947 India is divided into two countries, India and Pakistan, and both become independent.

2004 Giant tsunami destroys coastal areas of South Asia.

Mt. Everest is the world's highest mountain.
It is 29,028 feet (8,848 meters) high.

The Dead Sea is the lowest point on earth,
1,339 feet (408 meters) below sea level.

Lake Baikal in Russia is the deepest lake in
the world. Its greatest depth is slightly more
than a mile.

Russia's Kamchatka Peninsula is one of the most
volcanically active places in the world.

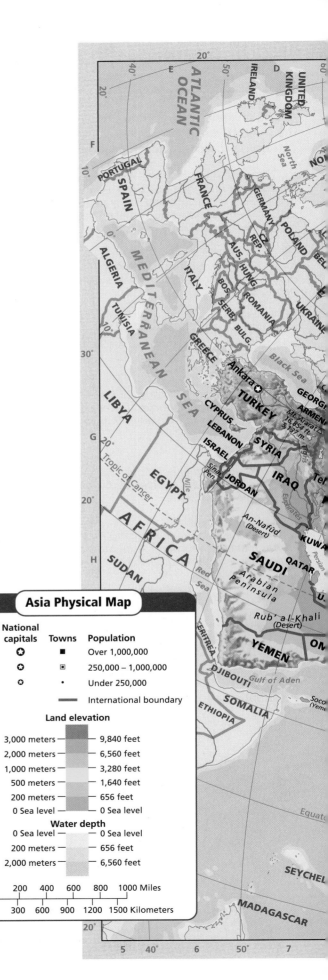

Asia Physical Map

National capitals	Towns	Population
✪	■	Over 1,000,000
✪	▣	250,000 – 1,000,000
✪	•	Under 250,000
	──	International boundary

Land elevation

3,000 meters	9,840 feet
2,000 meters	6,560 feet
1,000 meters	3,280 feet
500 meters	1,640 feet
200 meters	656 feet
0 Sea level	0 Sea level

Water depth

0 Sea level	0 Sea level
200 meters	656 feet
2,000 meters	6,560 feet

0   200   400   600   800   1000 Miles
0   300   600   900   1200   1500 Kilometers

ARCTIC OCEAN

North Pole

BARENTS SEA

KARA SEA

LAPTEV SEA

EAST SIBERIAN SEA

New Siberian Islands

North Siberian Lowland

Severnaya Zemlya

Novaya Zemlya

Yamal Pen.

Central Siberian Plateau

Verkhoyansk Mts.

BERING SEA

Kamchatka Peninsula

Aleutian Islands (U.S.)

RUSSIA

Ural Mountains

West Siberian Plain

S i b e r i a

Ob'

Yenisey

Angara

Stanovoy Mountains

Amur

SEA OF OKHOTSK

Sakhalin

Mys Lopatka

Novosibirsk

Lake Baikal

Sayan Mountains

Yablonovoy Range

Greater Khingan Range

Kuril Islands

Sikhote-Alin' (Mts.)

Tatar Strait

Hokkaidō

KAZAKHSTAN

Kazakh Hills

Altai Mountains

Selenge

Manchuria

SEA OF JAPAN

Honshū

JAPAN

Aral Sea

Lake Balkhash

Dzungarian Basin

MONGOLIA

Gobi Desert

NORTH KOREA

SOUTH KOREA

Fujisan 12,388 ft. 3,776 m.

Tōkyō

UZBEKISTAN

Syr Darya

Tien Shan

Beijing

Bo Hai

Korea Strait

Shikoku

Kyūshū

TURKMENISTAN

KYRGYZSTAN

TAJIKISTAN

Pamirs (Mts.)

Tarim Pendi (Basin)

Qilian Shan (Mts.)

Qaidam Pendi (Basin)

YELLOW SEA

EAST CHINA SEA

PACIFIC OCEAN

Tropic of Cancer

Amu Darya

K2 (Qogir Feng) 28,250 ft. △ 8,611 m.

Altun Shan (Mts.)

CHINA

Huang (Yellow)

Shanghai

AFGHANISTAN

Hindu Kush

Kunlun Mts.

Plateau of Tibet

Qin Ling (Mts.)

NORTHERN MARIANA ISLANDS (U.S.)

PAKISTAN

Himalayas

Szechwan Basin

GUAM (U.S.)

New Delhi

Mt. Everest 29,028 ft. △ 8,848 m.

NEPAL

Plateau of Yunnan

Nan Ling (Mts.)

Woyi Shan (Hills)

Philippine Sea

Great Indian Desert

BHUTAN

Brahmaputra

Ganges

Taiwan Strait

Kāthiāwār Peninsula

INDIA

BANGLA-DESH

Kolkata (Calcutta)

Luzon Strait

Mumbai (Bombay)

Godāvari

Deccan (Plateau)

Eastern Ghāts

Western Ghāts

MYANMAR

LAOS

Gulf of Tonkin

Hainan Dao

Luzon

Manila

PHILIPPINES

PALAU

Indochina

VIETNAM

SOUTH CHINA SEA

Mindanao

Bay of Bengal

THAILAND

CAMBODIA

Bangkok

Lakshadweep (India)

Andaman Islands (India)

Gulf of Thailand

Sulu Sea

Cape Comorin

SRI LANKA

Andaman Sea

Mui Ca Mau (Cape)

Celebes Sea

Moluccas

New Guinea

MALDIVES

Nicobar Islands (India)

Dondra Head

Str. of Malacca

MALAY PENINSULA

BRUNEI

MALAYSIA

Celebes

Ceram

Puncak Jaya △ 16,503 ft. 5,030 m.

MALAYSIA

SINGAPORE

Borneo

Banda Sea

Arafura Sea

Sumatra

Greater Sunda Islands

Java Sea

Lesser Sunda Is.

Timor

EAST TIMOR

AUSTRALIA

Gulf of Carpentaria

INDIAN OCEAN

N

W E

S

Jakarta

Java

INDONESIA

Timor Sea

© Rand McNally
Made in U.S.A.
N-CLA60000-A1- -5-6-9

70° 9 80° 10 90° 11 100° 12 110° 13 120° 14 130° 15 140°

The Republic of Indonesia is located in Southeast Asia. Only three countries in the world have more people than this country.

China is the world's most populous country. It is home to more than 1.3 billion people.

Kyrgyzstan is located in Central Asia. It became a country when the Soviet Union broke up in 1991.

Turkey is Asia's westernmost country. Istanbul, its largest city, lies along the Bosporus Strait, which divides Asia and Europe.

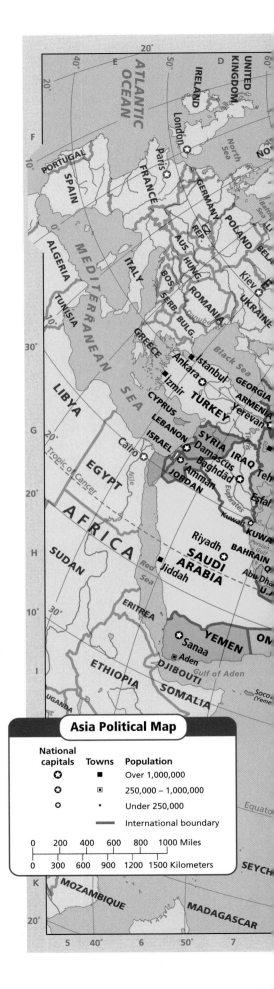

Asia Political Map

National capitals	Towns	Population
✪	■	Over 1,000,000
✪	▣	250,000 – 1,000,000
✪	·	Under 250,000
	▬	International boundary

0   200   400   600   800   1000 Miles
0   300   600   900   1200 1500 Kilometers

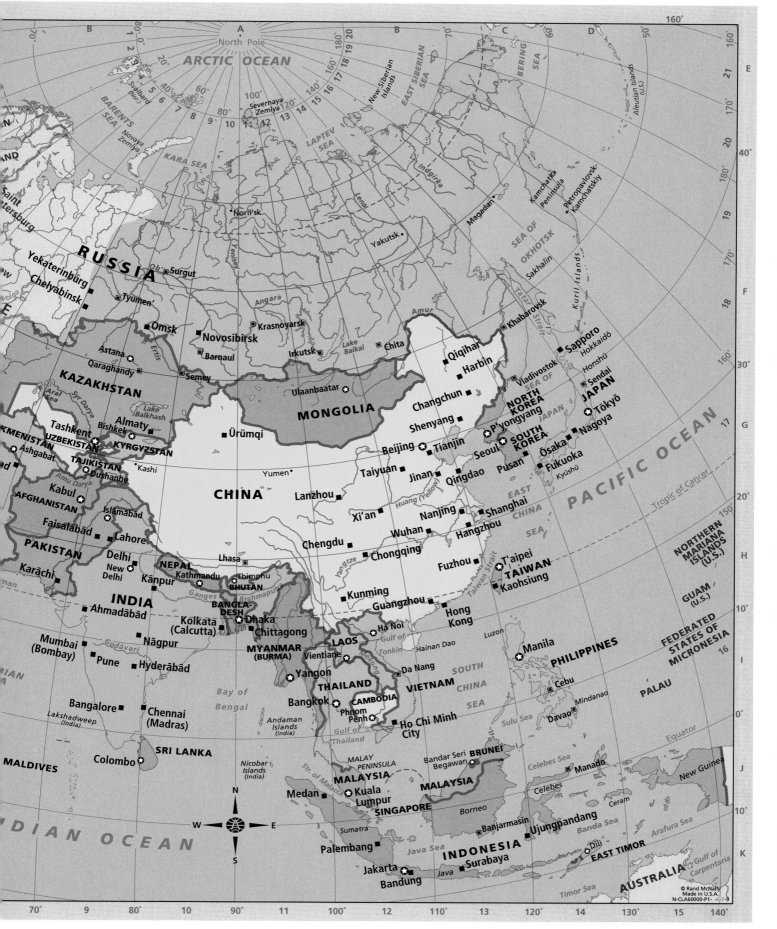

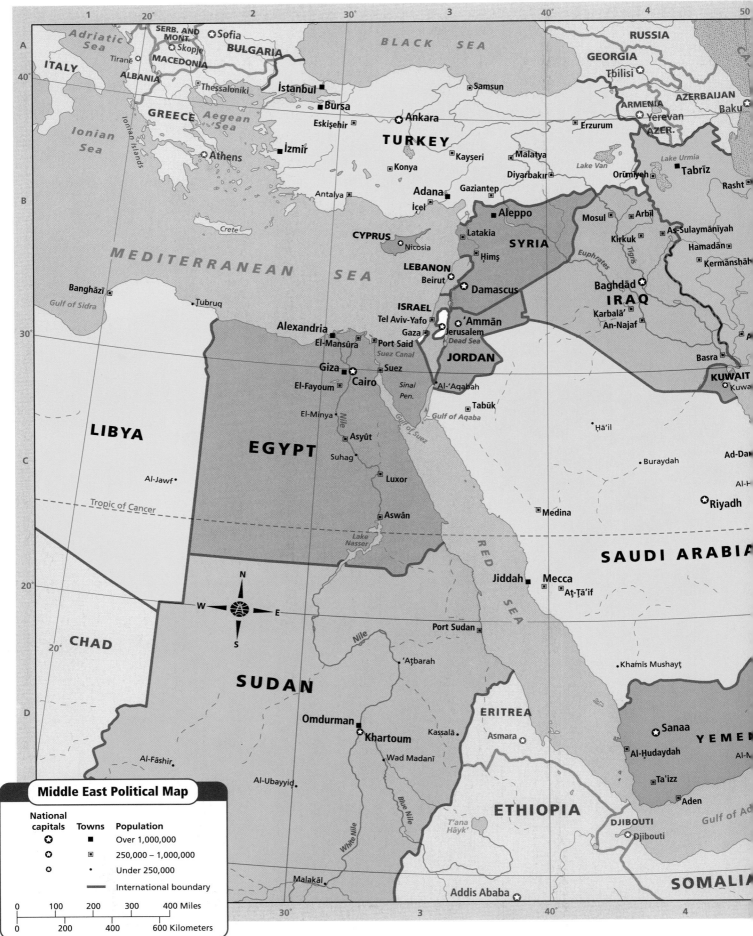

Middle East Political Map

National capitals	Towns	Population
⊛	■	Over 1,000,000
⊙	▣	250,000 – 1,000,000
⊙	•	Under 250,000
		▬ International boundary

0   100   200   300   400 Miles
0   200   400   600 Kilometers

The Middle East

Africa, Asia, and Europe meet in the Middle East. Since ancient times, great powerful empires have fought to control these lands, their resources, and their trade routes. Today, the oil that many of these countries produce is valuable to rich countries. There are also deep-rooted cultural conflicts among the peoples there.

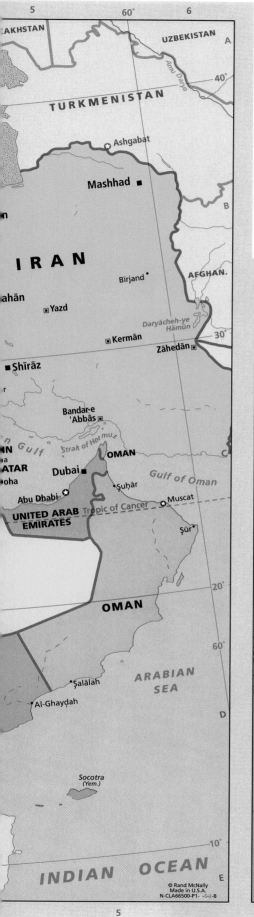

(A) Golan Heights. Occupied and unilaterally annexed by Israel.

(B) West Bank. Controlled by Israel, parts administered by the Palestinian Authority. Permanent status to be determined.

(C) Gaza Strip. Controlled by Israel, parts administered by the Palestinian Authority. Permanent status to be determined.

© Rand McNally
Made in U.S.A.
N-CLA66500-P1- -6-8-8

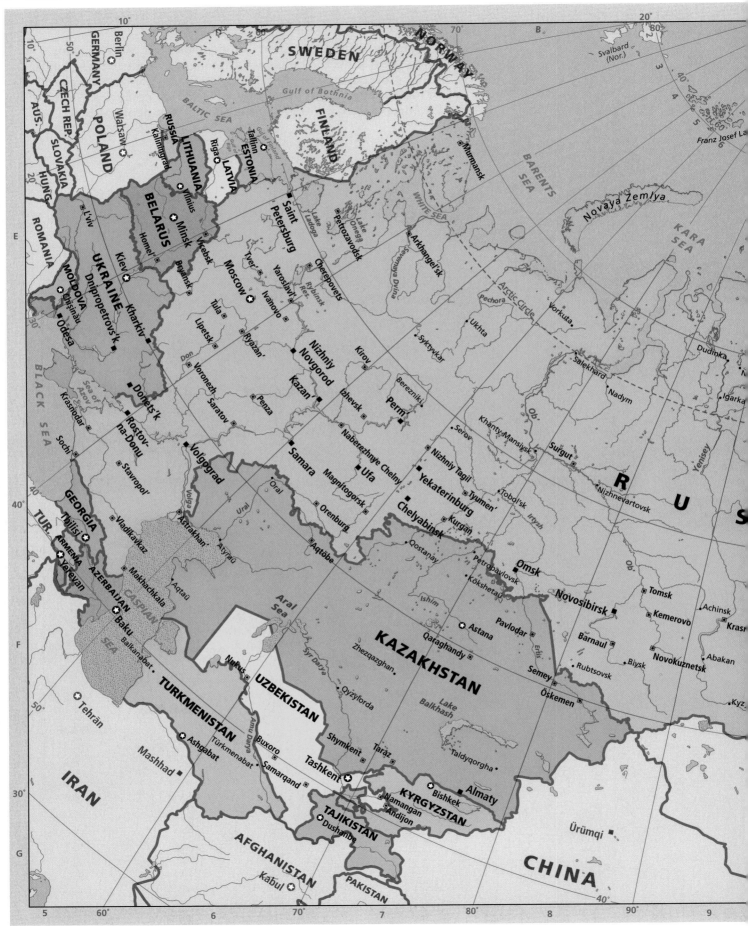

GERMANY
AUS.
CZECH REP.
SLOVAKIA
HUNG
POLAND
Warsaw
Berlin
ROMANIA
MOLDOVA
Chişinău
Odesa
UKRAINE
Kiev
L'viv
Dnipropetrovs'k
Kharkiv
Donets'k
Rostov-
na-Donu
Krasnodar
Sochi
Stavropol'
Sea of
Azov
BLACK SEA
GEORGIA
Tbilisi
TUR.
ARMENIA
Yerevan
AZERBAIJAN
Baku
Makhachkala
Vladikavkaz
Volgograd
Astrakhan'
Aqtaü
CASPIAN SEA
Balkanabat
TURKMENISTAN
Ashgabat
Türkmenabat
Tehrän
Mashhad
IRAN
AFGHANISTAN
Kabul
PAKISTAN

SWEDEN
NORWAY
Gulf of Bothnia
BALTIC SEA
FINLAND
LITHUANIA
Vilnius
Kaliningrad
RUSSIA
Riga
LATVIA
Tallinn
ESTONIA
Gulf of Finland
BELARUS
Minsk
Homel'
Vitebsk
Bryansk
Saint Petersburg
Lake Ladoga
Lake Onega
Cherepovets
Tver'
Yaroslavl'
Ivanovo
Rybinsk Res.
Moscow
Tula
Ryazan'
Lipetsk
Voronezh
Don
Saratov
Penza
Samara
Nizhniy Novgorod
Kazan'
Izhevsk
Naberezhnye Chelny
Ufa
Magnitogorsk
Orenburg
Oral
Ural
Volga
Atyraü
WHITE SEA
Murmansk
Arkhangel'sk
Severnaya Dvina
Syktyvkar
Ukhta
Pechora
Kirov
Berezniki
Perm'
Serov
Nizhniy Tagil
Yekaterinburg
Tyumen'
Kurgan
Chelyabinsk
Qostanay
Petropavlovsk
Kökshetaū
Aqtöbe
BARENTS SEA
Novaya Zemlya
KARA SEA
Svalbard (Nor.)
Franz Josef La
Arctic Circle
Vorkuta
Salekhard
Nadym
Dudinka
Igarka
Ob'
Irtysh
Tobol'sk
Khanty-Mansiysk
Surgut
Nizhnevartovsk
Yenisey
R U S
Omsk
Novosibirsk
Tomsk
Kemerovo
Krasn
Barnaul
Biysk
Rubtsovsk
Novokuznetsk
Abakan
Achinsk
Öskemen
Semey
Ertis
KAZAKHSTAN
Aral Sea
Nukus
UZBEKISTAN
Syr Darya
Amu Darya
Buxoro
Samarqand
Türkmenabat
Zhezqazghan
Qaraghandy
Astana
Pavlodar
Ishim
Qyzylorda
Shymkent
Taraz
Lake Balkhash
Taldyqorgha
Tashkent
Bishkek
Almaty
KYRGYZSTAN
Namangan
Andijon
TAJIKISTAN
Dushanbe
Ürümqi
CHINA
Kyz

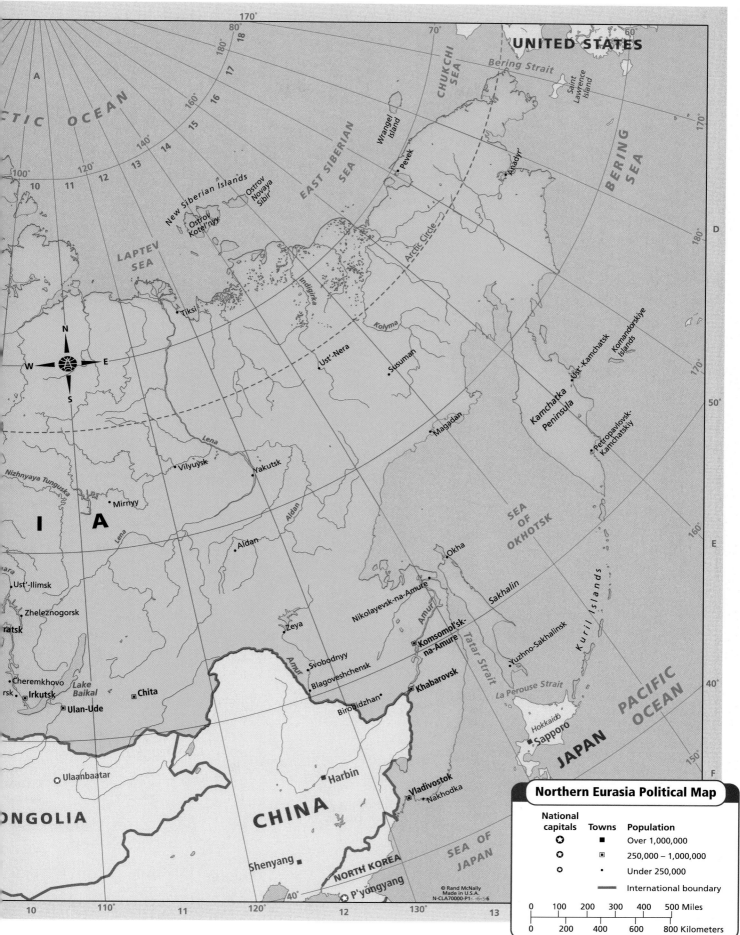

UNITED STATES

ARCTIC OCEAN

Bering Strait

CHUKCHI SEA

BERING SEA

Saint Lawrence Island

Wrangel Island

Pevek

Anadyr'

New Siberian Islands

Ostrov Novaya Sibir'

Ostrov Kotel'nyy

LAPTEV SEA

EAST SIBERIAN SEA

Arctic Circle

Tiksi

Indigirka

Kolyma

Ust'-Nera

Susuman

Komandorskiye Islands

Ust'-Kamchatsk

Kamchatka Peninsula

Petropavlovsk-Kamchatskiy

N W E S

Magadan

Lena

Vilyuysk

Yakutsk

Nizhnyaya Tunguska

Mirnyy

SEA OF OKHOTSK

I A

Lena

Aldan

Aldan

Okha

Sakhalin

Kuril Islands

Ust'-Ilimsk

Zheleznogorsk

ratsk

Zeya

Nikolayevsk-na-Amure

Amur

Komsomol'sk-na-Amure

Tatar Strait

Yuzhno-Sakhalinsk

Svobodnyy

Cheremkhovo

Lake Baikal

rsk

Irkutsk

Chita

Blagoveshchensk

Khabarovsk

La Perouse Strait

PACIFIC OCEAN

Ulan-Ude

Birobidzhan

Hokkaido

Sapporo

JAPAN

Ulaanbaatar

Harbin

Vladivostok

Nakhodka

MONGOLIA

CHINA

SEA OF JAPAN

Shenyang

NORTH KOREA

P'yongyang

© Rand McNally
Made in U.S.A.
N-CLA70000-P1- -6- -6

Northern Eurasia Political Map

National capitals	Towns	Population
⊙	■	Over 1,000,000
⊙	⊡	250,000 – 1,000,000
⊙	•	Under 250,000
	▬	International boundary

0 100 200 300 400 500 Miles

0 200 400 600 800 Kilometers

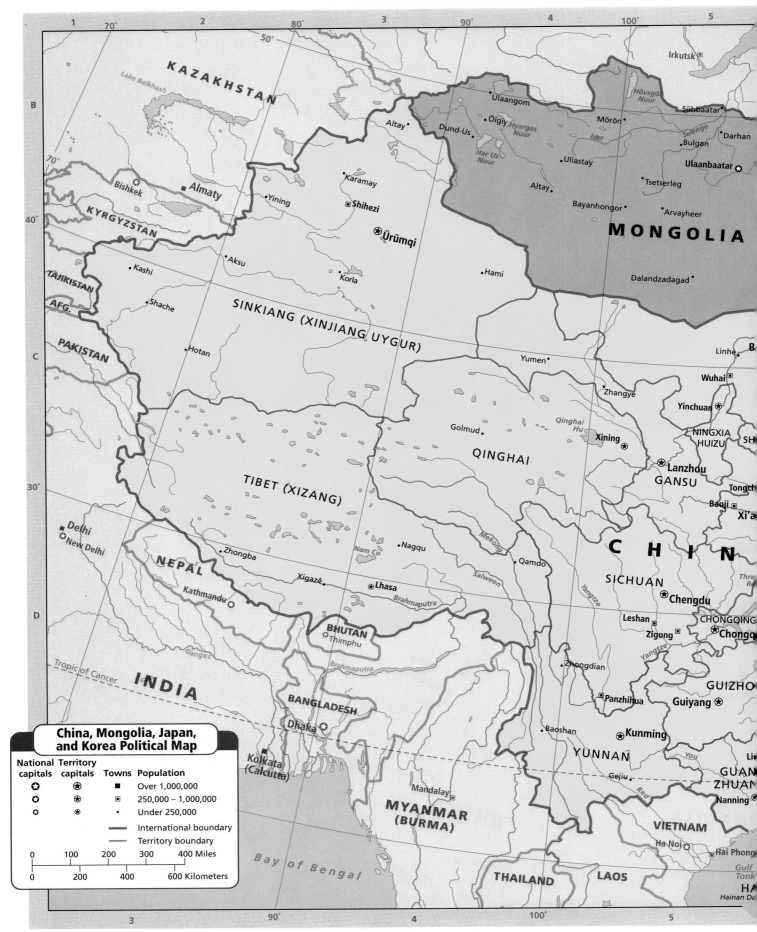

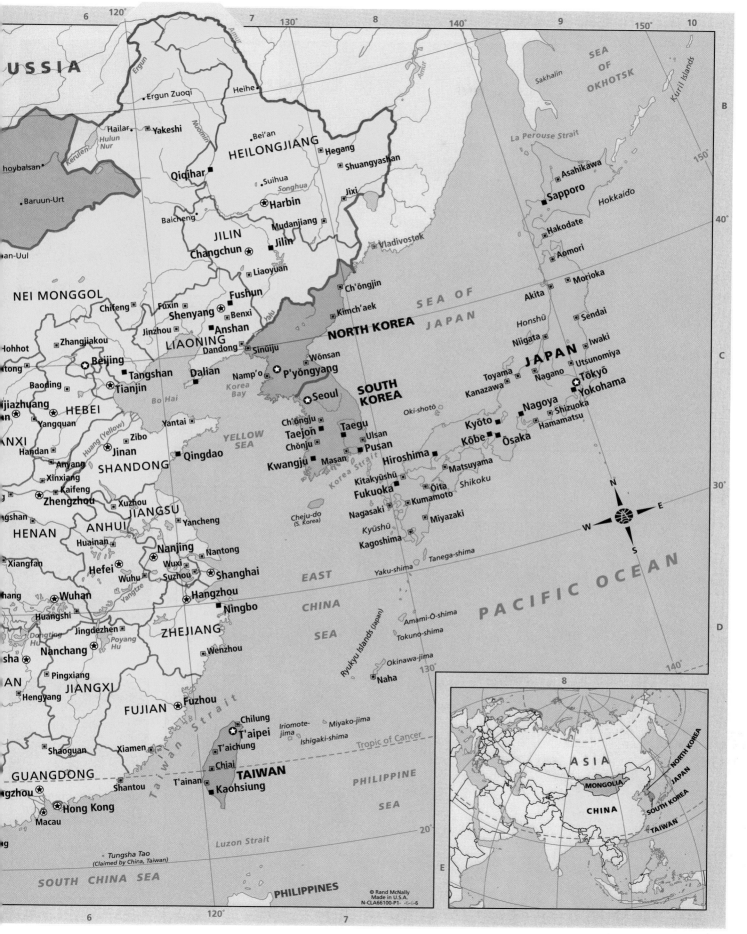

USSIA

6 120° 7 130° 8 140° 9 150° 10

Ergun

Amur

•Ergun Zuoqi •Heihe B

Hailar• Yakeshi Bei'an SEA OF OKHOTSK

Hulun Nur HEILONGJIANG Hegang Sakhalin Kuril Islands

Nuomin

hoybalsan• Qiqihar Shuangyashan La Perouse Strait 150°

Suihua Songhua Jixi Asahikawa

•Baruun-Urt Harbin Sapporo Hokkaidō 40°

Baicheng Mudanjiang Hakodate

JILIN Jilin Vladivostok Aomori

NEI MONGGOL Changchun Morioka

an-Uul Liaoyuan Ch'ŏngjin Akita

Fushun Kimch'aek SEA OF Niigata Sendai

Chifeng Fuxin Shenyang Benxi JAPAN Honshū Iwaki

Hohhot Zhangjiakou Jinzhou Anshan NORTH KOREA JAPAN Utsunomiya

•tong Baoding LIAONING Dandong Sinŭiju Wŏnsan Toyama Nagano Tōkyō

Beijing Tangshan Dalian Namp'o P'yŏngyang Kanazawa Yokohama

jiazhuang Tianjin Bo Hai Korea SOUTH Oki-shotō Nagoya Shizuoka

Yangquan HEBEI Bay Seoul KOREA Kyōto Hamamatsu

an XI Yantai Ch'ŏngju Taegu Kōbe Ōsaka

Handan Zibo YELLOW Taejŏn Ulsan

Anyang Jinan SEA Chŏnju Pusan Hiroshima Matsuyama

Xinxiang SHANDONG Qingdao Kwangju Masan Kitakyūshū Shikoku

Kaifeng Fukuoka Ōita

Zhengzhou Xuzhou Cheju-do Nagasaki Kumamoto

gshan JIANGSU Yancheng (S. Korea) Miyazaki

HENAN ANHUI Yanghou Kyūshū

Xiangfan Huainan Nanjing Nantong Kagoshima Tanega-shima

Hefei Wuxi Yaku-shima

Xhang Wuhu Suzhou Shanghai EAST

Wuhan Yangtze Hangzhou CHINA

Huangshi Ningbo SEA

Dongting Jingdezhen ZHEJIANG

sha Nanchang Poyang Hu Amami-Ō-shima

Pingxiang Wenzhou Tokuno-shima

AN JIANGXI Okinawa-jima

Hengyang FUJIAN Fuzhou Ryukyu Islands (Japan) Naha 130°

Taiwan Strait

Shaoguan Chilung Iriomote- Miyako-jima

Xiamen T'aipei jima

GUANGDONG Chiai Ishigaki-shima Tropic of Cancer

Shantou T'aichung TAIWAN PHILIPPINE

gzhou T'ainan SEA

Hong Kong Kaohsiung

Macau Luzon Strait 20°

g Tungsha Tao (Claimed by China, Taiwan)

SOUTH CHINA SEA PHILIPPINES

© Rand McNally
Made in U.S.A.
N-CLA66100-P1- -6-6-6

6 120° 7

Climate

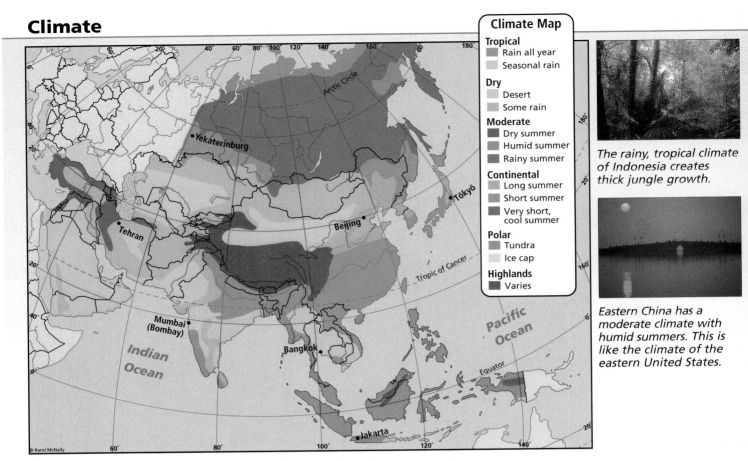

Climate Map

Tropical
- Rain all year
- Seasonal rain

Dry
- Desert
- Some rain

Moderate
- Dry summer
- Humid summer
- Rainy summer

Continental
- Long summer
- Short summer
- Very short, cool summer

Polar
- Tundra
- Ice cap

Highlands
- Varies

The rainy, tropical climate of Indonesia creates thick jungle growth.

Eastern China has a moderate climate with humid summers. This is like the climate of the eastern United States.

Economies

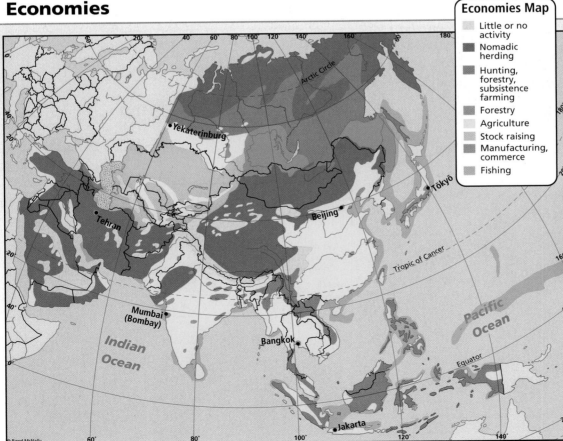

Economies Map
- Little or no activity
- Nomadic herding
- Hunting, forestry, subsistence farming
- Forestry
- Agriculture
- Stock raising
- Manufacturing, commerce
- Fishing

Rice is the most important food crop in Southeast Asia.

Japan sends many of its exports to the United States, but it trades with other countries, too. Trading with many countries helps a country continue to earn money if one trading partner has economic problems.

Population

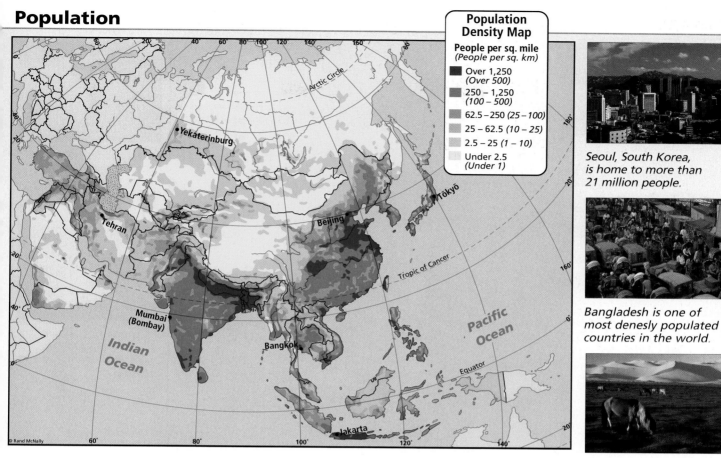

Population Density Map

People per sq. mile
(People per sq. km)

■	Over 1,250 *(Over 500)*
■	250 – 1,250 *(100 – 500)*
■	62.5 – 250 *(25 – 100)*
■	25 – 62.5 *(10 – 25)*
■	2.5 – 25 *(1 – 10)*
□	Under 2.5 *(Under 1)*

Seoul, South Korea, is home to more than 21 million people.

Bangladesh is one of most densely populated countries in the world.

Much of Mongolia is sparsely populated.

India and China

China and India are the world's population giants. Both have populations of more than one billion people. India's population, however, is growing faster. By 2040 it will be larger than China's. Since about 1980, China has strictly limited how many children a family may have and has brought down its rate of population growth.

India and China Population Growth

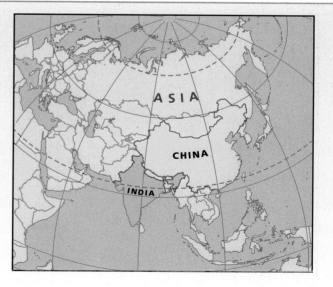

ASIA

CHINA

INDIA

Graph: y-axis labeled 2,000,000,000; 1,500,000,000; 1,000,000,000; 500,000,000; 0. x-axis labeled 1960 1970 1980 1990 2000 2010 2020 2030 2040 2050.

○ China
○ India

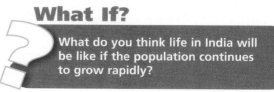

What If?

What do you think life in India will be like if the population continues to grow rapidly?

Transportation

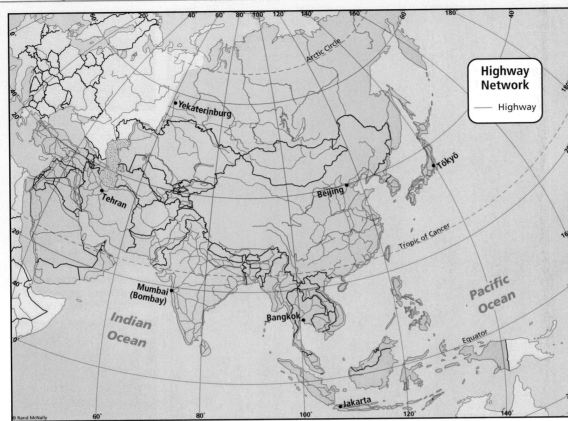

Japan's bullet trains can travel at speeds of up to 155 miles per hour (249 km/hr).

Mountainous terrain makes road-building difficult in many parts of Asia.

Environments

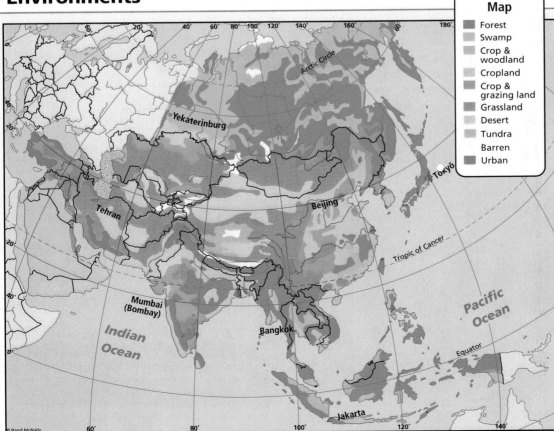

The country of Nepal lies along the southern edge of the Himalayas. Thick woodlands cover some of the lower elevations.

Grasslands called "steppes" cover much of Central Asia.

Natural Hazards

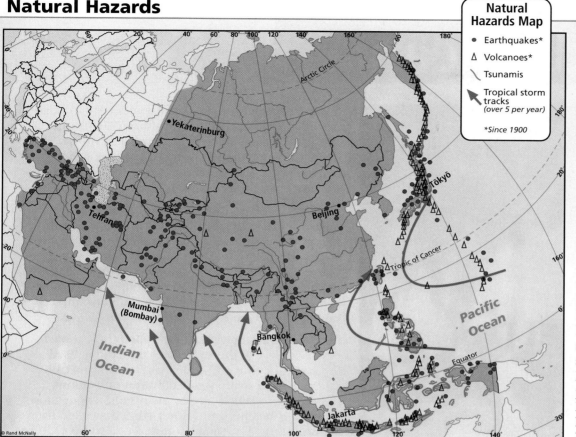

Natural Hazards Map
- • Earthquakes*
- △ Volcanoes*
- ╲ Tsunamis
- ◤ Tropical storm tracks *(over 5 per year)*

*Since 1900

Tsunamis

Tsunamis are huge ocean waves caused by underwater earthquakes or volcanoes. They usually travel at speeds of about 300 miles per hour (500 km/hr).

Tsunamis that reach the shore can cause terrible damage to coastal areas. On December 26, 2004, a strong earthquake off the coast of Sumatra in Indonesia caused a tsunami that destroyed huge coastal areas in Indonesia, Thailand, India, and Sri Lanka and also hit Madagascar and continental Africa. More than 200,000 people were killed. Most other tsunamis have occurred in the Pacific Ocean.

Energy

On the Mineral Fuel Deposits map, note the cluster of symbols indicating petroleum deposits around the Persian Gulf, which is near the left edge of the map. This area is part of the Middle East, which produces one-third of the world's oil.

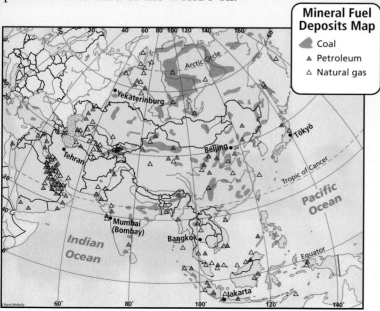

Mineral Fuel Deposits Map
- ◣ Coal
- ▲ Petroleum
- △ Natural gas

Oil exporting has brought great wealth to the countries in the Persian Gulf region of the Middle East. This photo shows an oil refinery in the United Arab Emirates.

An oil tanker and pipeline in Saudi Arabia.

China produces more than one-fourth of the world's coal.

Australia and Oceania

Uluru, also known as Ayers Rock, in central Australia.

Australia is the only continent except Antarctica that lies completely in the Southern Hemisphere. Oceania consists of New Zealand, part of the island of New Guinea, and thousands of other islands in the Pacific Ocean. Many of these islands are tiny coral atolls where no one lives. Others are the tops of volcanoes.

Australia is the smallest continent. It is about the size of the conterminous 48 U.S. states. Antarctica is the only continent that is drier than Australia. Because Australia is in the Southern Hemisphere, it is warmer in the north than in the south. New Zealand is made up of smaller islands, and it gets ample rainfall. New Guinea is warm and rainy all year.

Australia's vast, dry interior is called the Outback. Few people live there. Most of the land is used for grazing cattle and sheep on huge farms called "stations." For many years, children on stations have "gone to school" by two-way radio connection with their teachers and other students called the School of the Air. Today, computers also provide connections for such children.

Australia's first people are the Aborigines. They came to Australia from Asia thousands of years before the first Europeans came. People from Asia also settled other islands of Oceania. New Zealand was the last place they reached. English people started coming to Australia and New Zealand in the late 1700s. People from the British Isles still make up most of the population, but Asians and people from the Pacific Islands have joined them. In both Australia and New Zealand, most people live along the coasts in modern cities.

Sydney, Australia

Dairy farm on New Zealand's South Island

A Historical Look At Australia

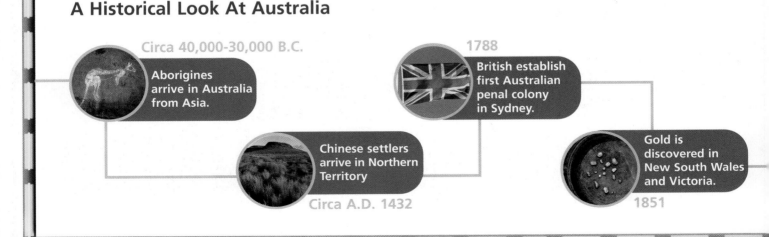

Circa 40,000-30,000 B.C.
Aborigines arrive in Australia from Asia.

Circa A.D. 1432
Chinese settlers arrive in Northern Territory

1788
British establish first Australian penal colony in Sydney.

1851
Gold is discovered in New South Wales and Victoria.

Australia's Extremes

Landforms Map
- Mountains
- Plains
- Hills and low tablelands

Indian Ocean

Gulf of Carpentaria

Coral Sea

Cape York Peninsula

Arnhem Land

Kimberley Plateau

Barkly Tableland

MACDONNELL RANGES

Great Sandy Desert

Simpson Desert

Gibson Desert

Great Victoria Desert

Great Artesian Basin

GREAT DIVIDING RANGE

Darling

Murray

Great Australian Bight

Tasman Sea

TASMANIA

© Rand McNally

Hottest recorded temperature:
Cloncurry, Queensland
128° F (53° C)

Largest freestanding monolith:
Uluru (Ayers Rock), Northern Territory
1,141.7 feet (348 m) high above ground by 2.2 miles (3.6 km) long by 1.5 miles (2.4 km) wide

Lowest point:
Lake Eyre, South Australia
52 feet (16 m) below sea level

Driest place:
Mulka, South Australia
4.05 inches (10 cm)/year

Longest river:
Murray River, southeastern Australia
1,566 miles (2,520 km)

Wettest place:
Bellenden Ker, Queensland
340 inches (863.6 cm) of precipitation a year

Longest coral reef:
Great Barrier Reef, northeast coast of Queensland
1,250 miles (2,000 km)

Highest point:
Mt. Kosciuszko, New South Wales
7,313 feet (2,229 m)

Coldest recorded temperature:
Charlotte Pass, New South Wales
-8° F (-22° C)

Largest island:
Tasmania
26,400 square miles (68,400 square km)

Marsupials of Australia

Australia's marsupials — pouched mammals — have survived because they have very few natural enemies. About half of Australia's 230 species of mammals are marsupials.

Koala

Wallabies

Tasmanian devil

Wombat

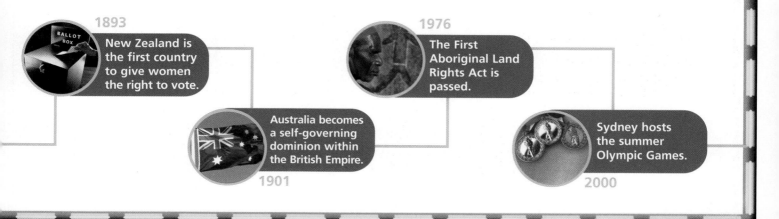

1893 New Zealand is the first country to give women the right to vote.

Australia becomes a self-governing dominion within the British Empire. **1901**

1976 The First Aboriginal Land Rights Act is passed.

Sydney hosts the summer Olympic Games. **2000**

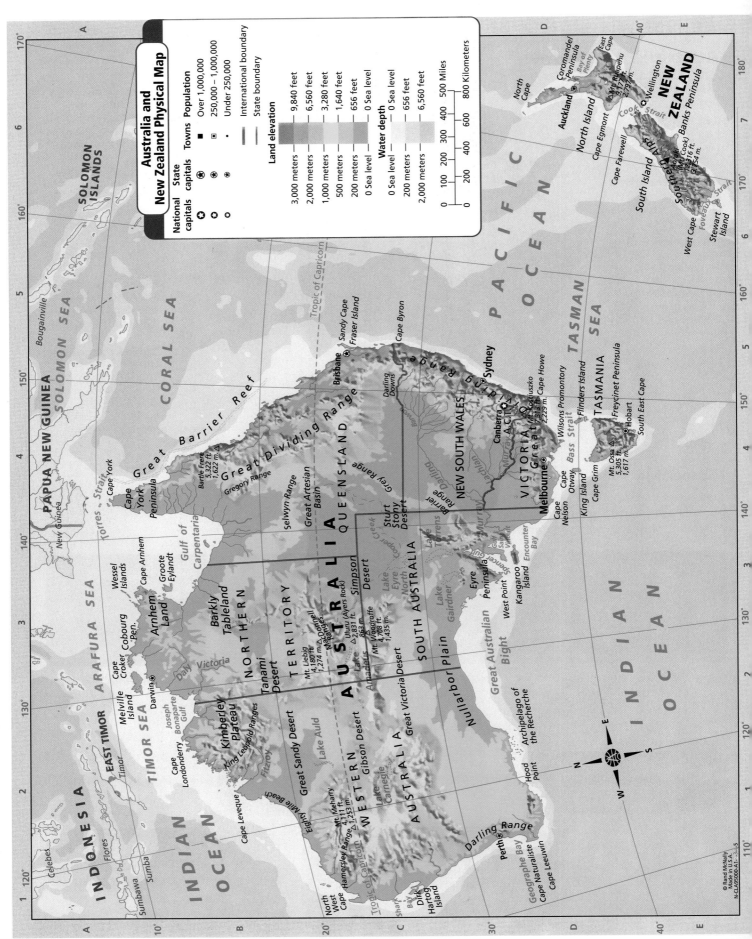

Australia and New Zealand Physical Map

Towns Population
- ■ Over 1,000,000
- ▣ 250,000 – 1,000,000
- • Under 250,000

International boundary
State boundary

	National capitals	State capitals
	⊛	⊛
	✪	✪

Land elevation

3,000 meters	9,840 feet
2,000 meters	6,560 feet
1,000 meters	3,280 feet
500 meters	1,640 feet
200 meters	656 feet
0 Sea level	0 Sea level

Water depth

0 Sea level	0 Sea level
200 meters	656 feet
2,000 meters	6,560 feet

500 Miles
800 Kilometers

© Rand McNally
Made in U.S.A.
N-CLA9500-A1-—5

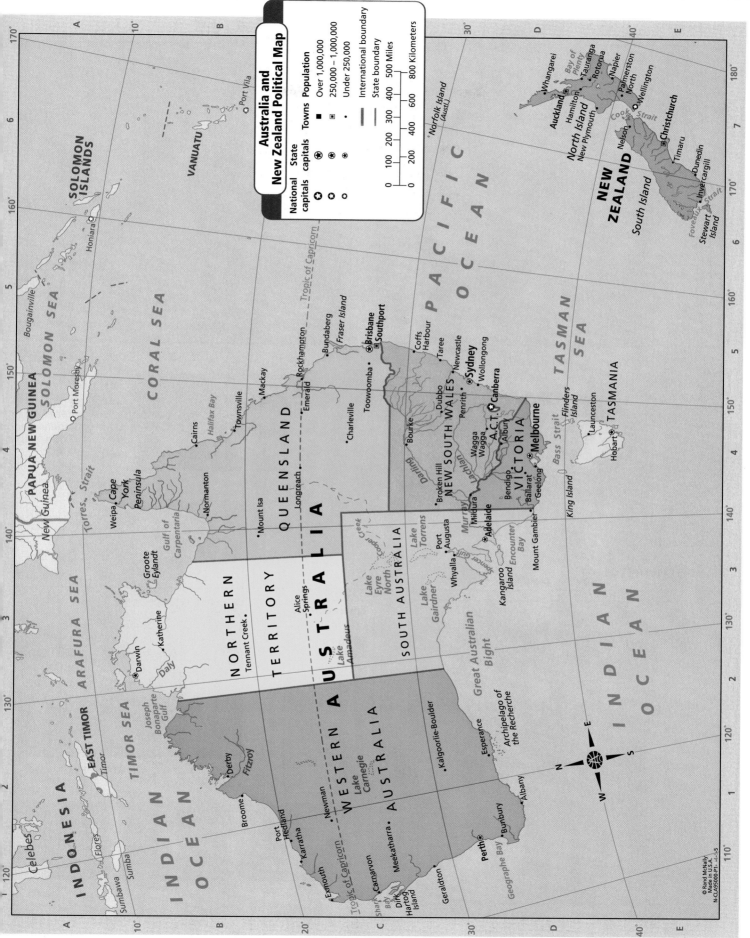

Australia and New Zealand Political Map

Towns Population
- Over 1,000,000
- 250,000 – 1,000,000
- Under 250,000

National capitals / State capitals

International boundary
State boundary

0 100 200 300 400 500 Miles
0 200 400 600 800 Kilometers

INDONESIA
Celebes
Flores
Sumba
Sumbawa
Timor
EAST TIMOR

PAPUA NEW GUINEA
New Guinea
Port Moresby

SOLOMON ISLANDS
Bougainville
Honiara

VANUATU
Port Vila

ARAFURA SEA
TIMOR SEA
Joseph Bonaparte Gulf
Darwin
Katherine
Daly

CORAL SEA
SOLOMON SEA
Torres Strait
Gulf of Carpentaria
Cape York Peninsula
Weipa
Groote Eylandt
Normanton
Cairns
Halifax Bay
Townsville
Mackay

PACIFIC OCEAN

Norfolk Island (Austl.)

NEW ZEALAND
Whangarei
Auckland
Hamilton
North Island
New Plymouth
Bay of Plenty
Tauranga
Rotorua
Napier
Palmerston North
Wellington
Nelson
Cook Strait
Christchurch
Timaru
South Island
Dunedin
Invercargill
Foveaux Strait
Stewart Island

INDIAN OCEAN

NORTHERN TERRITORY
Tennant Creek
Alice Springs
Lake Amadeus

QUEENSLAND
Tropic of Capricorn
Mount Isa
Longreach
Emerald
Charleville
Rockhampton
Bundaberg
Fraser Island
Toowoomba
Brisbane
Southport
Coffs Harbour
Taree
Newcastle

WESTERN AUSTRALIA
Broome
Derby
Fitzroy
Port Hedland
Karratha
Exmouth
Newman
Meekatharra
Lake Carnegie
Carnarvon
Shark Bay
Dirk Hartog Island
Geraldton
Geographe Bay
Bunbury
Perth
Albany
Kalgoorlie-Boulder
Esperance
Archipelago of the Recherche
Tropic of Capricorn

SOUTH AUSTRALIA
Cooper Creek
Lake Eyre North
Lake Torrens
Lake Gairdner
Port Augusta
Whyalla
Spencer Gulf
Kangaroo Island
Adelaide
Encounter Bay
Mount Gambier
Great Australian Bight

NEW SOUTH WALES
Darling
Bourke
Broken Hill
Dubbo
Penrith
Sydney
Wollongong
Lachlan
Wagga Wagga
A.C.T.
Canberra
Albury
Murray
Mildura
Murrumbidgee

VICTORIA
Bendigo
Ballarat
Geelong
Melbourne

Bass Strait
King Island
Flinders Island
Launceston
TASMANIA
Hobart

TASMAN SEA

N E S W

© Rand McNally
Made in U.S.A.
N-CLA95000-P1-4-5

Climate

Transportation

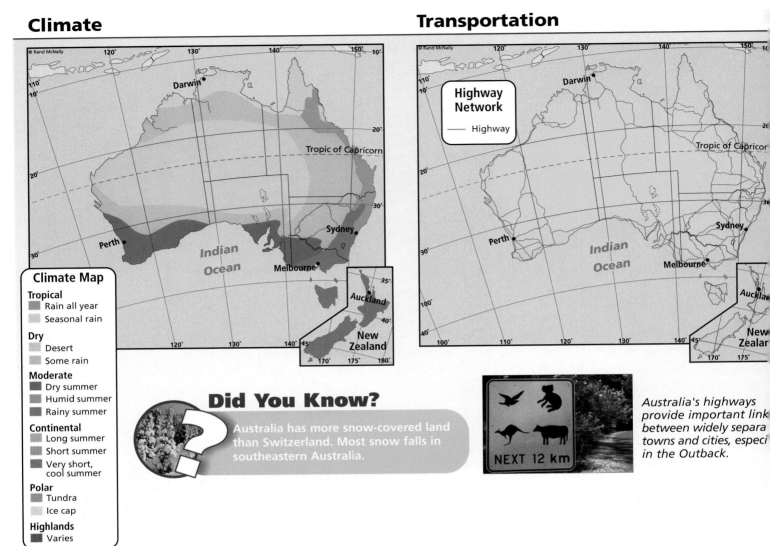

Climate Map

Tropical
- Rain all year
- Seasonal rain

Dry
- Desert
- Some rain

Moderate
- Dry summer
- Humid summer
- Rainy summer

Continental
- Long summer
- Short summer
- Very short, cool summer

Polar
- Tundra
- Ice cap

Highlands
- Varies

Highway Network
— Highway

Did You Know?

Australia has more snow-covered land than Switzerland. Most snow falls in southeastern Australia.

Australia's highways provide important link between widely separa towns and cities, especi in the Outback.

Environments

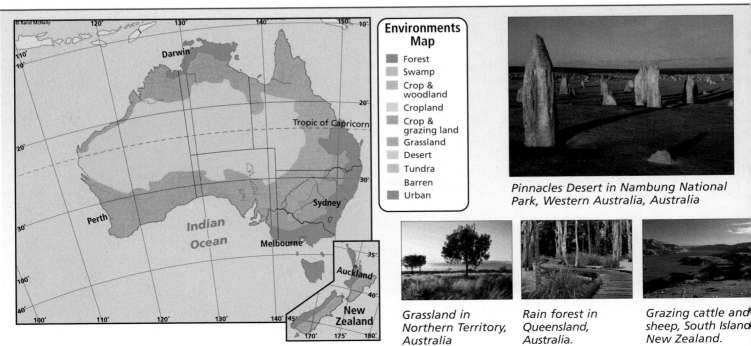

Environments Map
- Forest
- Swamp
- Crop & woodland
- Cropland
- Crop & grazing land
- Grassland
- Desert
- Tundra
- Barren
- Urban

Pinnacles Desert in Nambung National Park, Western Australia, Australia

Grassland in Northern Territory, Australia

Rain forest in Queensland, Australia.

Grazing cattle and sheep, South Island New Zealand.

Economies

Population

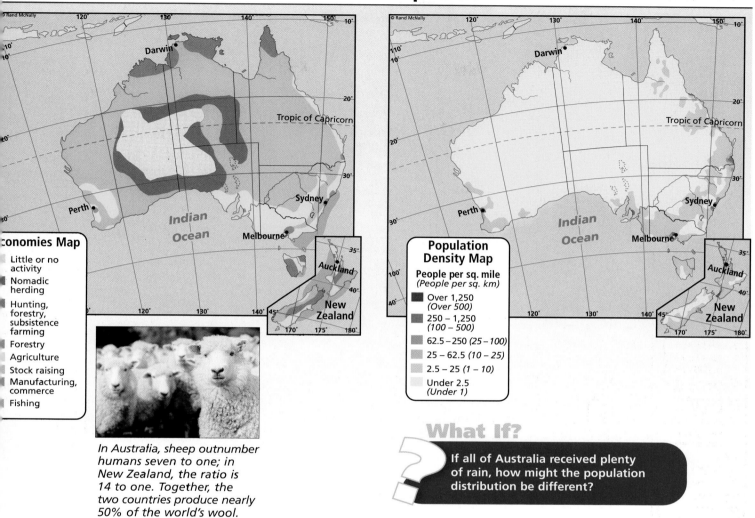

Economies Map

- Little or no activity
- Nomadic herding
- Hunting, forestry, subsistence farming
- Forestry
- Agriculture
- Stock raising
- Manufacturing, commerce
- Fishing

Population Density Map

People per sq. mile
(People per sq. km)

- Over 1,250 *(Over 500)*
- 250 – 1,250 *(100 – 500)*
- 62.5 – 250 *(25 – 100)*
- 25 – 62.5 *(10 – 25)*
- 2.5 – 25 *(1 – 10)*
- Under 2.5 *(Under 1)*

In Australia, sheep outnumber humans seven to one; in New Zealand, the ratio is 14 to one. Together, the two countries produce nearly 50% of the world's wool.

What If?

?

If all of Australia received plenty of rain, how might the population distribution be different?

The Great Barrier Reef

The Great Barrier Reef stretches for roughly 1,250 miles (2,000 km) along the northeast coast of Queensland, Australia. It is made up of more than 2,600 separate coral reefs. Together, they cover 80,000 square miles (207,200 square kilometers). The Great Barrier Reef is the largest group of coral reefs and islands in the world.

Scientists believe that the reef began forming millions of years ago. More than 400 different types of coral, in a great variety of colors, form the reef. In addition, about 1,500 species of fish live in the warm waters around the reef. Scientists warn that some human activities are causing serious damage to the reef.

More than 600 islands can be found along the Great Barrier Reef. Some of them have been developed as tourist resorts.

Maori wrasse

Whale shark

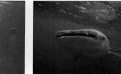

Acropora plate coral

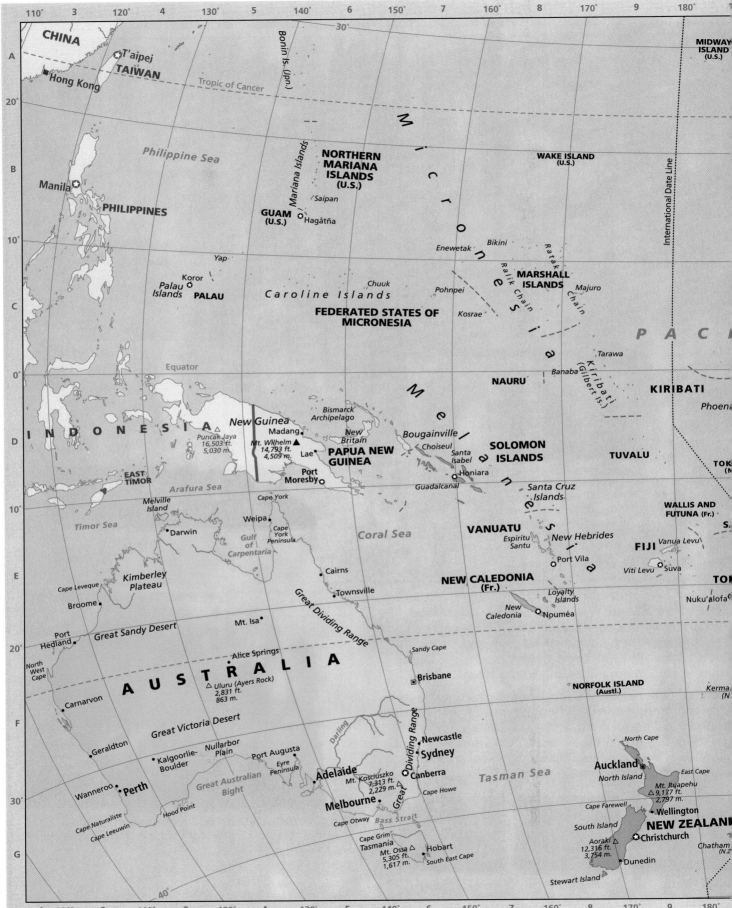

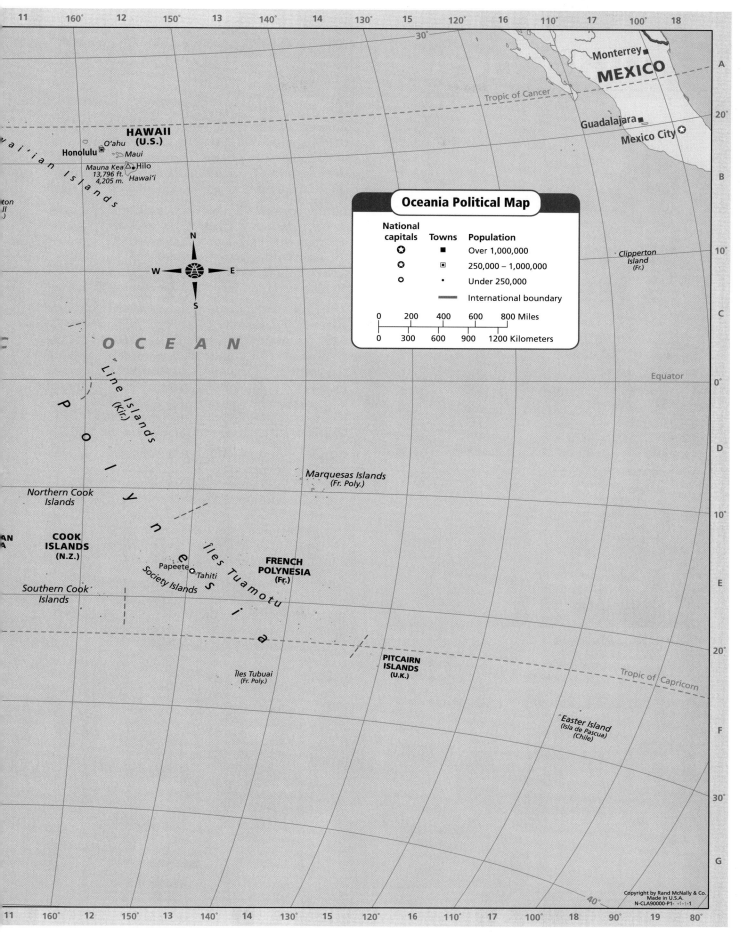

11 | 160° | 12 | 150° | 13 | 140° | 14 | 130° | 15 | 120° | 16 | 110° | 17 | 100° | 18

A

30°

Monterrey ■

MEXICO

Tropic of Cancer

20°

Guadalajara ■

Mexico City ⊛

HAWAII (U.S.)

O'ahu

Honolulu □ ≈ Maui

Mauna Kea △ Hilo
13,796 ft.
4,205 m. Hawai'i

B

ton

ll)

10°

Clipperton
Island
(Fr.)

Oceania Political Map

National capitals	Towns	Population
⊛	■	Over 1,000,000
✪	▣	250,000 – 1,000,000
⊙	•	Under 250,000
	▬	International boundary

0   200   400   600   800 Miles

0   300   600   900   1200 Kilometers

N
W ✦ E
S

O C E A N

C

Line Islands
(Kir.)

Equator 0°

P

D

Marquesas Islands
(Fr. Poly.)

Northern Cook
Islands

10°

**COOK
ISLANDS
(N.Z.)**

o
l
y
n
e
s
i
a

Papeete ⊙ Tahiti

Society Islands

Îles Tuamotu

**FRENCH
POLYNESIA
(Fr.)**

E

Southern Cook
Islands

AN

A

Îles Tubuai
(Fr. Poly.)

**PITCAIRN
ISLANDS
(U.K.)**

20°

Tropic of Capricorn

Easter Island
(Isla de Pascua)
(Chile)

F

30°

G

40°

11 | 160° | 12 | 150° | 13 | 140° | 14 | 130° | 15 | 120° | 16 | 110° | 17 | 100° | 18 | 90° | 19 | 80°

Antarctica

Kayaking in sea ice along the Antarctic coast.

Antarctica is the world's fifth largest continent. Most of it lies within the Antarctic Circle. It is the world's most isolated landmass: The nearest land is the southern tip of South America, about 700 miles (more than 1,100 km) from the Antarctic Peninsula.

All the land within the Antarctic Circle has days in winter when the sun never rises and days in summer when the sun never sets. At the South Pole, the six months from March 20 until September 21 have continuous darkness, and the six months from September 21 to March 20 have continuous daylight.

Antarctica is the coldest place on earth. Average summer temperatures may reach only about 0° F (-18° C). Such a cold, frozen landmass produces cold winds that collide with warmer air around the coast and form a belt of storms. Antarctica receives very little precipitation. What precipitation does fall produces ice, which accumulates into ice sheets that gradually push toward the coast and form ice shelves over the edge of the land.

People discovered Antarctica only about 200 years ago. Exploration on land started a little more than 100 years ago. No people live on Antarctica permanently. Several countries support scientists who study global climate change and the atmosphere's thinning ozone layer as well as plant and animal life. A few tourists visit the continent each year.

Scientists know that the continent has such resources as coal, but an international agreement prohibits exploiting these resources. Perhaps the most important resources are the abundant life in the cold waters off the coast.

Passengers crowd the deck of an icebreaker ship as it plows through pack ice.

Exploring a huge crevasse on Ross Island.

A Historical Look At Antarctica

1819-1821 Fabian von Bellingshausen, a Russian, is the first European to see Antarctica.

1894 A Norwegian expedition is the first to land on Victoria Land.

1911 Roald Amundsen is the first person to reach the South Pole.

1929 Richard Byrd flies over the South Pole.

Scientific Stations in Antarctica

Frozen and isolated as it is, Antarctica offers some important advantages for researchers. Its darkness makes it a good place to study the stars. Its clean air allows studies of air quality. Scientists can see the effects of human activity. Antarctica has no borders, so scientists from different countries can share the information they find.

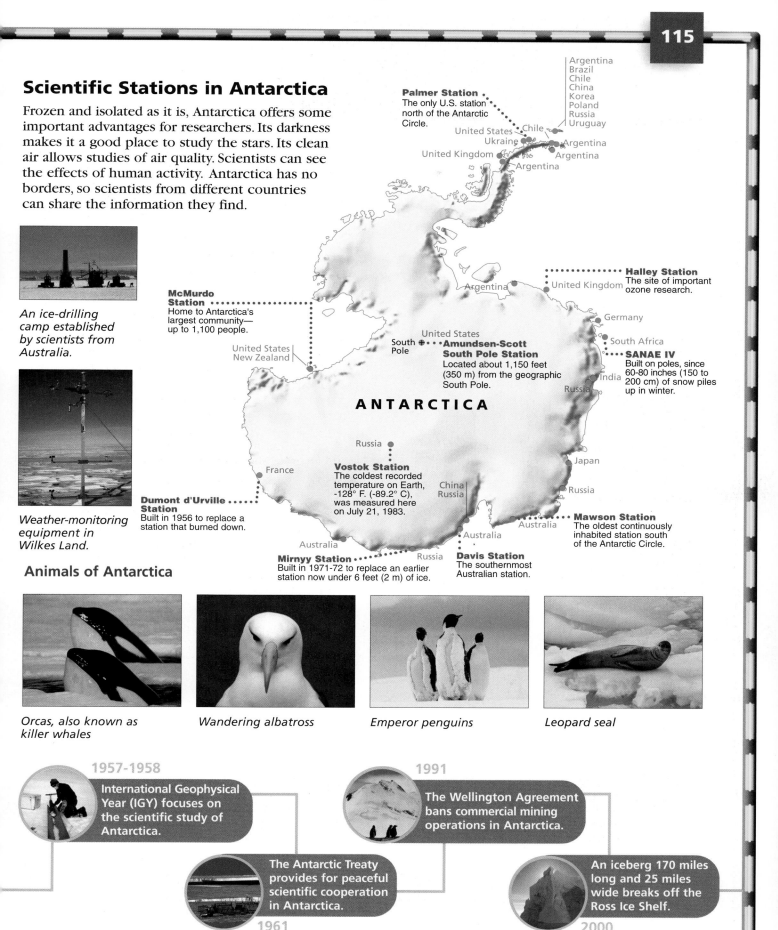

An ice-drilling camp established by scientists from Australia.

Weather-monitoring equipment in Wilkes Land.

Palmer Station
The only U.S. station north of the Antarctic Circle.

Argentina
Brazil
Chile
China
Korea
Poland
Russia
Uruguay

United States — Chile
Ukraine — Argentina
United Kingdom — Argentina
Argentina

Halley Station
The site of important ozone research.

United Kingdom

Germany

South Africa

SANAE IV
Built on poles, since 60-80 inches (150 to 200 cm) of snow piles up in winter.

India

Russia

McMurdo Station
Home to Antarctica's largest community—up to 1,100 people.

United States
New Zealand

United States
South Pole

Amundsen-Scott South Pole Station
Located about 1,150 feet (350 m) from the geographic South Pole.

ANTARCTICA

Russia

Japan

Vostok Station
The coldest recorded temperature on Earth, -128° F. (-89.2° C), was measured here on July 21, 1983.

China
Russia

France

Dumont d'Urville Station
Built in 1956 to replace a station that burned down.

Australia

Australia

Australia

Russia

Mawson Station
The oldest continuously inhabited station south of the Antarctic Circle.

Mirnyy Station
Built in 1971-72 to replace an earlier station now under 6 feet (2 m) of ice.

Davis Station
The southernmost Australian station.

Argentina

Animals of Antarctica

Orcas, also known as killer whales

Wandering albatross

Emperor penguins

Leopard seal

1957-1958
International Geophysical Year (IGY) focuses on the scientific study of Antarctica.

1991
The Wellington Agreement bans commercial mining operations in Antarctica.

The Antarctic Treaty provides for peaceful scientific cooperation in Antarctica.

1961

An iceberg 170 miles long and 25 miles wide breaks off the Ross Ice Shelf.

2000

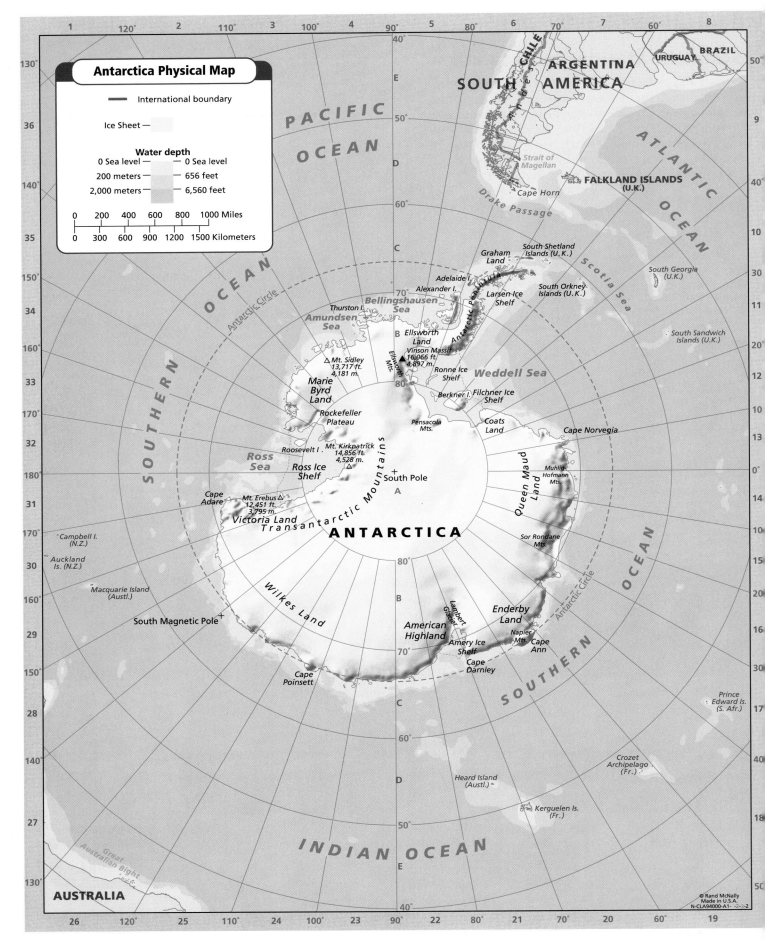

Antarctica Physical Map

— International boundary

Ice Sheet —

Water depth

0 Sea level —	— 0 Sea level
200 meters —	— 656 feet
2,000 meters —	— 6,560 feet

0 200 400 600 800 1000 Miles
0 300 600 900 1200 1500 Kilometers

PACIFIC OCEAN

SOUTHERN OCEAN

SOUTH AMERICA

ARGENTINA

CHILE

URUGUAY

BRAZIL

Strait of Magellan

Cape Horn

Drake Passage

FALKLAND ISLANDS (U.K.)

ATLANTIC OCEAN

Scotia Sea

South Georgia (U.K.)

South Shetland Islands (U.K.)

Graham Land

Adelaide I.

Alexander I.

Larsen Ice Shelf

South Orkney Islands (U.K.)

South Sandwich Islands (U.K.)

Antarctic Circle

Thurston I.

Bellingshausen Sea

Amundsen Sea

Ellsworth Land

Vinson Massif 16,066 ft. 4,897 m.

Ellsworth Mts.

Ronne Ice Shelf

Weddell Sea

Berkner I.

Filchner Ice Shelf

Mt. Sidley 13,717 ft. 4,181 m.

Marie Byrd Land

Rockefeller Plateau

Pensacola Mts.

Coats Land

Cape Norvegia

Roosevelt I.

Mt. Kirkpatrick 14,856 ft. 4,528 m.

Ross Sea

Ross Ice Shelf

Queen Maud Land

Muhlig-Hofmann Mts.

South Pole

ANTARCTICA

Transantarctic Mountains

Cape Adare

Mt. Erebus 12,451 ft. 3,795 m.

Victoria Land

Sor Rondane Mts.

Campbell I. (N.Z.)

Auckland Is. (N.Z.)

South Magnetic Pole

Wilkes Land

Lambert Glacier

American Highland

Enderby Land

Napier Mts.

Cape Ann

Amery Ice Shelf

Cape Darnley

Macquarie Island (Austl.)

SOUTHERN OCEAN

Antarctic Circle

Prince Edward Is. (S. Afr.)

Cape Poinsett

Crozet Archipelago (Fr.)

Heard Island (Austl.)

Kerguelen Is. (Fr.)

INDIAN OCEAN

Great Australian Bight

AUSTRALIA

© Rand McNally
Made in U.S.A.
N-CLA94000-A1--2-3-2

hematic Content Index

is index makes it easy to compare different continents and regions of the world in terms of climate,
onomies, and other major themes covered in the atlas.

The Oceans of the World

Rank	Ocean	Area sq. miles	Area sq. kilometers
1	Pacific Ocean	60,100,000	155,557,000
2	Atlantic Ocean	29,600,000	76,762,000
3	Indian Ocean	26,500,000	68,556,000
4	Southern Ocean	7,800,000	20,327,000
5	Arctic Ocean	5,400,000	14,056,000

The 10 Largest Islands

Rank	Island	Location	Area sq. miles	Area sq. kilometers
1	Greenland	North America	840,000	2,175,600
2	New Guinea	Asia-Oceania	308,900	800,000
3	Borneo	Asia	287,300	744,100
4	Madagascar	Africa	226,600	587,000
5	Baffin Island	North America	195,928	507,452
6	Honshū	Asia	89,176	230,966
7	Great Britain	Europe	88,795	229,978
8	Victoria Island	North America	83,897	217,291
9	Celebes	Asia	73,057	189,216
10	South Island	Oceania	57,708	149,463

The 10 Largest Lakes by Surface Area

Rank	Lake	Location	Length sq. miles	Length sq. kilometers
1	Caspian Sea	Asia-Europe	144,400	374,000
2	Lake Superior	North America	31,700	82,103
3	Lake Victoria	Africa	26,564	68,800
4	Lake Huron	North America	23,000	59,570
5	Lake Michigan	North America	22,300	57,757
6	Aral Sea	Asia	13,000	33,670
7	Lake Tanganyika	Africa	12,355	31,999
8	Lake Baikal	Asia	12,162	31,499
9	Great Bear Lake	North America	12,096	31,329
10	Lake Nyasa	Africa	11,120	28,801

The 10 Largest Lakes by Amount of Water

Rank	Lake	Location	Average volume of water cubic mi.	Average volume of water cubic km
1	Caspian Sea	Asia-Europe	18,800	78,200
2	Lake Baikal	Asia	5,700	23,600
3	Lake Tanganyika	Africa	4,600	19,000
4	Lake Superior	North America	2,900	12,100
5	Lake Nyasa	Africa	1,865	7,775
6	Lake Michigan	North America	1,180	4,920
7	Lake Huron	North America	849	3,540
8	Lake Victoria	Africa	662	2,760
9	Great Bear Lake	North America	550	2,292
10	Great Slave Lake	North America	501	1,738

Compare!

Lake Baikal is only the 8th largest lake in the world. However, because it is so deep, it holds more water than any lake except the Caspian Sea.

The 10 Deepest Lakes

Rank	Lake	Location	Greatest depth feet	Greatest depth meters
1	Lake Baikal	Asia	5,369	1,637
2	Lake Tanganyika	Africa	4,708	1,435
3	Caspian Sea	Asia-Europe	3,104	946
4	Lake Nyasa	Africa	2,316	706
5	Lake Issyk-Kul	Asia	2,297	700
6	Great Slave Lake	North America	2,015	614
7	Crater Lake	North America	1,943	592
8	Lake Tahoe	North America	1,685	514
9	Lake Chelan	North America	1,419	433
10	Great Bear Lake	North America	1,356	413

Compare!

Six of the world's ten deepest lakes are also among the ten largest lakes.

The 10 Longest Rivers

Rank	River	Location	Length miles	Length kilometers
1	Nile	Africa	4,132	6,650
2	Amazon	South America	4,000	6,437
3	Yangtze	Asia	3,915	6,301
4	Mississippi	North America	3,710	5,971
5	Plata-Paraná	South America	2,920	4,699
6	Huang (Yellow)	Asia	2,902	4,670
7	Mekong	Asia	2,796	4,500
8	Lena	Asia	2,734	4,400
9	Congo	Africa	2,715	4,369
10	Mackenzie	North America	2,635	4,241

Compare!

Four of the world's ten longest rivers are in Asia, the largest continent.

The 10 Rivers with the Greatest Amount of Water

Rank	River	Location	Average volume of water cubic mi.	Average volume of water cubic km.
1	Amazon	South America	1,661	6,923
2	Ganges	Asia	333	1,386
3	Congo	Africa	317	1,320
4	Orinoco	South America	242	1,007
5	Yangtze	Asia	241	1,006
6	Río de la Plata	South America	195	811
7	Yenisey	Asia	148	618
8	Lena	Asia	129	539
9	Mississippi	North America	122	510
10	Mekong	Asia	121	505

Compare!

The Amazon River has almost five times more water than any other river in the world.

The 10 Largest Countries

Rank	Country	Location	Area sq. miles	Area sq. kilometers
1	Russia	Europe-Asia	6,592,849	17,075,400
2	Canada	North America	3,855,103	9,984,670
3	United States	North America	3,794,083	9,826,630
4	China	Asia	3,690,045	9,557,172
5	Brazil	South America	3,300,172	8,547,404
6	Australia	Oceania	2,969,910	7,692,030
7	India	Asia	1,222,510	3,166,285
8	Argentina	South America	1,073,519	2,780,400
9	Kazakhstan	Asia	1,049,156	2,717,300
10	Sudan	Africa	967,500	2,505,813

Compare!

Russia, the world's largest country, is more than 70% larger than Canada, the second-largest.

The 10 Countries with the Greatest Population

Rank	Country	Location	Population
1	China	Asia	1,298,720,000
2	India	Asia	1,057,415,000
3	United States	North America	291,680,000
4	Indonesia	Asia	236,680,000
5	Brazil	South America	183,080,000
6	Pakistan	Asia	152,210,000
7	Russia	Europe-Asia	144,310,000
8	Bangladesh	Asia	139,875,000
9	Nigeria	Africa	135,570,000
10	Japan	Asia	127,285,000

Compare!

The United States and China are roughly the same size, but China has more than four times as many people.

Index of Abbreviations

The following abbreviations are used in the index.

Afr. . . . Africa
Austr. . . . Australia
cap. . . . capital
Can. . . . Canada
dep. . . . dependency
Eur. . . . Europe
Mex. . . . Mexico
mts. . . . mountains
N.A. . . . North America
Terr. . . . Territory or Territories
S.A. . . . South America
U.A. Emirates . . . United Arab Emirates
U.K. . . . United Kingdom
U.S. . . . Unites States

Index

Review "How to Use the Atlas" pages 4 and 5 for information on using an index.

Place	Map Key	Page
A		
Aberdeen, *South Dakota*	B6	**38**
Abidjan, *cap. Cote d'Ivoire, Afr.*	E3	**85**
Abilene, *Texas*	E6	**38**
Absaroka Range, *U.S.*	B3	**36**
Abu Dhabi, *cap. U. A. Emirates, Asia*	C5	**97**
Abuja, *cap. Nigeria, Afr.*	E4	**85**
Acapulco, *Guerrero, Mexico*	C3	**62**
Accra, *cap. Ghana, Afr.*	E3	**85**
Aconcagua, *Cerro, highest peak, S.A.*	G4	**68**
Adana, *Turkey*	B3	**96**
Ad-Dammām, *Saudi Arabia*	C5	**96**
Addis Ababa, *cap. Ethiopia, Afr.*	E7	**85**
Adelaide, *cap. South Australia, Austr.*	D3	**109**
Aden, *Yemen*	D4	**96**
Aden, Gulf of, *Afr./Asia*	H6	**92**
Adirondack Mountains, *U.S.*	C11	**37**
Adriatic Sea, *Europe*	C5	**74**
Aegean Sea, *Europe*	D6	**75**
Afghanistan, *country, Asia*	F8	**95**
Aguascalientes, *cap. Ags., Mex.*	B2	**62**
Aguascalientes, *state, Mexico*	B2	**62**
Ahaggar, *mts., Algeria*	C4	**84**
Ahmadābād, *India*	G9	**95**
Ahvāz, *Iran*	B4	**96**
Akita, *Japan*	C9	**101**
'Akko, *Israel*	g10	**97**
Akron, *Ohio*	C9	**39**
Alabama, *state, U.S.*	E8	**39**
Alamogordo, *New Mexico*	E4	**38**
Al-'Aqabah, *Jordan*	C3	**96**
Alaska, *state, U.S.*	B6	**40**
Alaska, Gulf of, *N.A.*	D7	**40**
Alaska Peninsula, *Alaska*	D5	**40**
Alaska Range, *Alaska*	C6	**40**
Albania, *country, Eur.*	C5	**76**
Albany, *Georgia*	E9	**39**
Albany, *cap. New York, U.S.*	C11	**39**
Albany River, *Canada*	C9	**55**
Alberta, *province, Canada*	C6	**56**
Albuquerque, *New Mexico*	D4	**38**
Aleppo, *Syria*	B3	**96**
Aleutian Islands, *Alaska*	f15	**40**
Aleutian Range, *Alaska*	D6	**40**
Alexandria, *Egypt*	B3	**96**
Algeria, *country, Afr.*	C4	**85**
Algiers, *cap. Algeria, Afr.*	B4	**85**
Alice Springs, *Australia*	C3	**109**
Allegheny Plateau, *U.S.*	C10	**37**
Allentown, *Pennsylvania*	C10	**39**
Almaty, *Kazakhstan*	E7	**98**
Alps, *mts., Eur.*	C4	**74**
Altai Mountains, *Asia*	E10	**93**
Altamaha River, *U.S.*	E9	**37**
Altun Shan, *mts., China*	F10	**93**
Al-Ubayyiḍ, *Sudan*	D3	**96**
Amarillo, *Texas*	D5	**38**
Amazon Basin, *S.A.*	D4	**68**
Amazon River, *S.A.*	D5	**68**
American Samoa, *dep., Oceania*	E11	**113**
Ammān, *cap. Jordan, Asia*	B3	**96**
Amsterdam, *cap. Netherlands, Eur.*	B4	**76**
Amu Darya, *river, Asia*	F8	**93**
Amundsen Sea, *Antarctica*	B2	**116**
Amur River, *Asia*	D12	**99**
Anchorage, *Alaska*	C7	**40**
Andaman Islands, *India*	H11	**93**
Andes, *mts., S.A.*	F4	**68**
Andorra, *country, Eur.*	C4	**76**
Angara River, *Russia*	D10	**99**
Angarsk, *Russia*	D10	**99**
Angel Falls, *S.A.*	C4	**68**
Angola, *country, Afr.*	G5	**85**
Anguilla, *dep., N.A.*	C6	**63**
Anhui, *province, China*	C6	**101**
Ankara, *cap. Turkey, Asia*	B3	**96**
Ann Arbor, *Michigan*	C9	**39**
Annapolis, *cap. Maryland, U.S.*	D10	**39**
Anshan, *China*	B7	**101**
Antalya, *Turkey*	B3	**96**
Antananarivo, *cap. Madagascar, Afr.*	G8	**85**
Antarctic Peninsula, *Antarctica*	B7	**116**
Anticosti, Île d', *island, Québec, Can.*	D11	**55**
Antigua and Barbuda, *country, N.A.*	C6	**63**
Antofagasta, *Chile*	F4	**69**
Anyang, *China*	C6	**101**
Aomori, *Japan*	B9	**101**
Apennines, *mts., Italy*	C5	**74**
Apia, *cap. Samoa, Oceania*	E10	**112**
Appalachian Mountains, *U.S.*	D9	**37**
Appleton, *Wisconsin*	C8	**39**
Aqaba, Gulf of, *Asia*	C3	**96**
Aqtaū, *Kazakhstan*	E5	**98**
Aqtöbe, *Kazakhstan*	D5	**98**
Arabian Peninsula, *Asia*	G6	**92**
Arabian Sea, *Afr./Asia*	H8	**93**
Arafura Sea, *Asia/Oceania*	A3	**108**
Aral Sea, *Asia*	E6	**98**
Arbīl, *Iraq*	B4	**96**
Arctic Ocean	A2	**11**
Argentina, *country, S.A.*	G4	**69**
Arica, *Chile*	E4	**69**
Arizona, *state, U.S.*	E3	**38**
Arkansas, *state, U.S.*	E7	**39**
Arkansas River, *U.S.*	D5	**36**
Arkhangel'sk, *Russia*	A8	**77**
Armenia, *country, Asia*	E4	**98**
Arnhem Land, *region, Austr.*	B3	**108**
Aruba, *country, N.A.*	C6	**63**
Arviat, *Nunavut, Canada*	B8	**57**
Asahikawa, *Japan*	B9	**101**
Ascension, *dep., Afr.*	F2	**85**
Ashdod, *Israel*	h9	**97**
Asheville, *North Carolina*	D9	**39**
Ashgabat, *cap. Turkmenistan, Asia*	F5	**98**
Ashqelon, *Israel*	h9	**97**
Asmara, *cap. Eritrea, Afr.*	D7	**85**
As-Salṭ, *Jordan*	g10	**97**
Astana, *cap. Kazakhstan, Asia*	D7	**98**
Astrakhan', *Russia*	C8	**77**
Asunción, *cap. Paraguay, S.A.*	F5	**69**
Aswân, *Egypt*	C3	**96**
Asyût, *Egypt*	C3	**96**
Athabasca, Lake, *Canada*	C7	**54**
Athens, *Georgia*	E9	**39**
Athens, *cap. Greece, Eur.*	D6	**77**
Atlanta, *cap. Georgia, U.S.*	E9	**39**
Atlantic City, *New Jersey*	D11	**39**
Atlantic Ocean	E9	**10**
Atlas Mountains, *Afr.*	B3	**84**
At-Tā'if, *Saudi Arabia*	C4	**96**
Auckland, *New Zealand*	D7	**109**
Augusta, *Georgia*	E9	**39**
Augusta, *cap. Maine, U.S.*	C12	**39**
Aurora, *Illinois*	C8	**39**
Austin, *cap. Texas, U.S.*	E6	**38**
Austria, *country, Eur.*	C5	**76**
Azerbaijan, *country, Asia*	E4	**98**
Azores, *dep., Eur.*	D11	**12**
Azov, Sea of, *Europe*	C7	**75**
B		
Baffin Bay, *N.A.*	A11	**55**
Baffin Island, *Nunavut, Can.*	A10	**55**
Baghdād, *cap. Iraq, Asia*	B4	**96**
Bahamas, *country, N.A.*	B5	**63**
Bahrain, *country, Asia*	C5	**97**
Baie-Comeau, *Québec, Canada*	D11	**57**
Baikal, Lake, *Russia*	D10	**99**
Baja California, *state, Mexico*	B1	**62**
Baja California Sur, *state, Mexico*	B1	**62**
Baker Lake, *Nunavut, Can.*	B8	**56**
Bakersfield, *California*	D2	**38**
Baku, *cap. Azerbaijan, Eur.*	E4	**98**
Balkan Peninsula, *Eur.*	C6	**74**
Balkhash, Lake, *Kazakhstan*	E7	**98**
Baltic Sea, *Eur.*	B5	**74**
Baltimore, *Maryland*	D10	**39**
Bamako, *cap. Mali, Afr.*	D3	**85**
Bandar-e 'Abbās, *Iran*	C5	**97**
Bandar Seri Begawan, *cap. Brunei, Asia*	I13	**95**
Bandung, *Indonesia*	J12	**95**
Bangalore, *India*	H9	**95**
Banghāzī, *Libya*	B6	**85**
Bangkok, *cap. Thailand, Asia*	H12	**95**
Bangladesh, *country, Asia*	G10	**95**
Bangor, *Maine*	C12	**39**
Bangui, *cap. Central African Republic, Afr.*	E5	**85**
Banjarmasin, *Indonesia*	J13	**95**
Barbados, *country, N.A.*	C7	**63**
Barcelona, *Spain*	C4	**76**
Bari, *Italy*	C5	**76**
Barkly Tableland, *Austr.*	B3	**108**
Barnaul, *Russia*	D8	**98**
Barquisimeto, *Venezuela*	C4	**69**
Barranquilla, *Colombia*	B3	**69**
Barrie, *Ontario, Canada*	D10	**57**
Barrow, *Alaska*	A5	**40**
Basra, *Iraq*	B4	**96**
Basseterre, *cap. Saint Kitts-Nevis, N.A.*	C6	**63**
Baton Rouge, *cap. Louisiana, U.S.*	E7	**39**
Beaufort Sea, *N.A.*	B6	**30**
Beaumont, *Texas*	E7	**39**
Beersheba, *Israel*	h9	**97**
Beijing, *cap. China, Asia*	C6	**101**
Beira, *Mozambique*	G7	**85**
Beirut, *cap. Lebanon, Asia*	B3	**96**
Belarus, *country, Eur.*	B6	**77**